How to Publish a
#1 Bestseller and
Impact Millions

I0457896

WRITE THE BOOK THAT CHANGES EVERYTHING

Samantha Moonsammy
Simar Nounou

✿ LUCKY BOOK PUBLISHING

Copyright © 2025 Samantha Moonsammy and Simar Nounou

❇ LUCKY BOOK PUBLISHING

Published by Lucky Book Publishing: LuckyBookPublishing.com

All rights reserved. No part of this book may be reproduced or used in any manner without the prior written permission of the copyright owner, except for the use of brief quotations in a book review.

The author does not dispense medical advice or prescribe the use of any technique as a form of treatment for physical, emotional or medical problems without the advice of a physician, either directly or indirectly. The intent of the author is only to offer information of a general true nature to help you in your quest for emotional, physical, and spiritual well-being. In the event you use any of the information in this book for yourself, the author and the publisher assume no responsibility for your actions.

To request permissions, contact the publisher at hello@luckybookpublishing.com.

Paperback ISBN: 978-1-997775-47-8
Hardcover ISBN: 978-1-997775-49-2
E-book ISBN: 978-1-997775-48-5

First edition, November 2025

book publishing for entrepreneurs; how to write a bestselling nonfiction book; build your brand with a book; business book writing guide; how to turn your book into a business; personal branding for authors; write the book grow your business; how to market your book and brand; legacy and impact entrepreneurship; creative business and storytelling strategy

DEDICATION

To every person who said "I've always wanted to write a book but...": this is for you. The "but" ends now. Your story matters. Your expertise is needed. Your voice deserves to be heard.

"You're ready now.
Write the book you keep talking about at dinner
parties, in your journal, in your head at 2am.
You've thought about it enough.
Dreamed about it enough.
The purpose, the love, the abundance you want are
on the other side of your resistance.
One sentence today. One paragraph tomorrow.
That's it. Start now."

– Samantha Moonsammy
Co-founder, Lucky Book Publishing

YOUR EXCLUSIVE BOOK BONUSES

As our gift to you, enjoy FREE access to the **Write the Book That Changes Everything digital bundle** - including the PDF of this book, the complete audiobook, author templates, and exclusive resources to help you write, publish, and promote your own bestselling book.

Simply scan the QR code below or visit
luckybookpublishing.com/book

Because when one of us writes the book that changes everything, it creates a ripple effect that inspires the world.

"When you write your book, you don't just change your life, you create opportunities, impact, and a legacy that lasts forever.
The world is waiting for your voice.
Start today."

– Simar Nounou
Co-founder, Lucky Book Publishing

PREFACE
Your Story Matters

Dear Reader,

We see you. We understand you.

You have a message inside you that won't let go. A book idea that keeps tugging at your heart. Maybe it's scribbled across sticky notes, half-written in a Google Doc, or tucked away in a notebook you keep meaning to open "When life slows down."

We know that feeling. The juggling act of business, family, deadlines, and dreams. The voice that says, "I'll start when I have more time." But somehow, "later" turns into months, even years, and those brilliant ideas stay trapped inside you.

You're not alone.
Eight out of ten people say they want to write a book. Less than one percent actually do.

But here's the truth we NEED you to hear.
Your story matters.

Your words will heal, help, and ignite change.
Your lessons will outlive you.
The ripple effect of your book and impact will reach farther than you can imagine.
To readers you will never meet, in places you will never go, changing lives you will never know about.

We wrote this book for you—the thought leader, the change-maker, the quiet visionary who's ready to be seen and heard. For the person who didn't grow up seeing people like them on New York City billboards in Times Square, on bestseller lists, or center stage as keynote speakers.

For the woman who knows she's meant for more.
For the person who's ready to step into purpose.
For the dreamer who's finally ready to do it.

It's your time to make this happen.
It's time to write your #1 bestseller and impact millions.
And you don't have to do this alone.
We've built the roadmap. We've tested the system.
We've gathered a community of authors ready to support and cheer you on.

Together, we will help you:
Write the Book.
Build the Business.
Be the Brand.

We are your book coaches, your accountability partners, your biggest cheerleaders. We'll challenge you to show up, to keep writing, and to finish what you started. Because your future readers are waiting.

This book isn't just about publishing. It's about purpose. It's about stepping into the next level of who you were always meant to be.

Welcome to the beginning of everything that's about to change.

With love and belief in your story,

Samantha and Simar
Co-Founders, Lucky Book Publishing
LuckyBookPublishing.com

AUTHOR'S NOTE
The Truth About Writing

Before we dive in, let's get real about what it takes to write the book that changes everything.

Here's the truth: You don't become a writer by learning about writing.

You become a writer by writing.

The system we've shared removes the mystery, eliminates the overwhelm, and provides a clear path. But the system doesn't write the book. You do.

We remember the first version of this book vividly. Samantha started and stopped seventeen times. Seventeen different Chapter Ones, each more perfect than the last, none of them leading to Chapter Two. She was waiting for the perfect opening, the perfect voice, the perfect moment when writing would feel easy and natural.

That moment never came. What came instead was a deadline, a speaking engagement where Samantha and

Simar promised to have copies of their book available. Eight weeks to write, edit, design, and print a book that existed only as seventeen different beginnings.

Samantha wrote Chapter One (version eighteen) on a Monday. It wasn't perfect. She wrote Chapter Two on Tuesday anyway. By Friday, we had five imperfect chapters that actually existed instead of one perfect chapter that didn't. The book was done in six weeks. Was it perfect? No. Did it help hundreds of people? Yes. Did those people care that some sentences could have been more elegant? Not one of them mentioned it.

We figured it out. Now, it's your turn to join us on this journey.

That's the real secret: You don't need to be perfect to make an impact. You just need to start.

Writing your book isn't about being the best writer, it's about being brave enough to share what you've lived, learned, and discovered. It's about choosing progress over perfection, and courage over comfort.

You don't have to do this alone. We'll walk this journey with you, word by word, chapter by chapter, as you step into the next version of yourself, the author version.

So take a deep breath. Let's begin this together.

Write the book, build the business, be the brand.

Contents

INTRODUCTION
Your Book Is Waiting

Your Book Is the Billboard That Builds Your Brand

Every year, four million books are published worldwide. That number might sound overwhelming, but here's what we've learned after helping hundreds of authors: Your book, the one sitting inside you right now, isn't just a creative project. It's the most powerful business development tool you'll ever create.

We're Samantha and Simar, co-founders of Lucky Book Publishing, and we've developed a system that takes the mystery out of writing and publishing. Not because we're naturally gifted writers (we're not), but because we discovered something powerful: **Your book is the cornerstone of everything. Your authority, your business growth, and your personal brand.**

Think of it this way: **Write the book, build the business,**

be the brand.

The journey that brought us here wasn't linear. Samantha spent years producing events for thought leaders, watching brilliant minds share transformative ideas from stages around the world. She worked with people like the late Wayne Dyer, Elizabeth Gilbert, Deepak Chopra, and Eckhart Tolle, observing how ideas could ripple through audiences, changing lives in real time. But she also saw something troubling: For every person on stage, there were hundreds in the audience with equally powerful messages, trapped by the belief that publishing was for "other people," the chosen few with connections, credentials, or extraordinary luck.

What Samantha noticed was that the people ON the stages had books. The people in the audience who wanted to BE on those stages? They didn't. The book was the differentiator. Not talent, not expertise, not even experience. The book opened the doors.

Simar came from a different angle, building businesses in the digital space, watching entrepreneurs struggle to establish authority in crowded markets. She saw people with decades of expertise losing opportunities to those who simply knew how to package and share their knowledge effectively. The traditional publishing gatekeepers weren't interested in these practical experts unless they already had massive platforms. Self-publishing existed, but it felt like being thrown into the ocean without a life jacket.

When we met, these two perspectives collided into a single realization: **A book isn't the end goal. It's the beginning of a business transformation.**

Your Book as a Business Asset

Let's get real about what a book does for your business:

It positions you as THE expert. When someone Googles your name and sees you've written a book, you instantly have more credibility than 99% of your competitors. You literally wrote the book on your topic.

It replaces years of traditional marketing. One book can do the work of hundreds of blog posts, dozens of speaking engagements, and countless networking meetings. It works for you 24/7.

It opens doors that stay closed to everyone else. Podcast hosts LOVE interviewing authors. Conference organizers seek out published experts. Media outlets want to quote people who've written books. These opportunities lead directly to clients, partnerships, and revenue.

It creates multiple income streams. Your book itself generates income, yes. But it also leads to speaking fees, consulting contracts, coaching programs, and courses. One of our authors calls it "replacing all your marketing with one book."

One of our authors, a consultant who'd been struggling to break into the corporate market, published her book on leadership. Within six months, she'd been invited to speak at three Fortune 500 companies. Her speaking fee? $15,000 per engagement. Her book investment? Less than $10,000. And those speaking gigs led to a $250,000 consulting contract. The book didn't just pay for itself, it became her most valuable business asset.

The Three Pillars: Book, Business, Brand

This book is built around a simple but powerful framework:

Write the Book: We'll show you exactly how to get your expertise out of your head and onto the page. No more staring at blank screens. No more wondering if you're "doing it right." You'll have a clear system that works.

Build the Business: Your book becomes the engine for business growth. We'll show you how to use your book to attract ideal clients, command higher fees, and create offers that people beg to buy.

Be the Brand: Your book establishes you as a recognizable authority. We'll show you how to leverage your published author status to become the go-to expert in your field, the one everyone wants to work with.

These three pillars support each other. Your book builds your business. Your business strengthens your brand. Your brand sells more books and attracts better clients.

It's a virtuous cycle that compounds over time.

This Isn't Just Theory

Everything in this book is based on real results from real authors. Like:

- **Michelle Weger**, bestselling author of *Don't Snooze Your Dreams: Lessons from Life with Narcolepsy*. Her story of pursuing your dreams despite disability has made her a sought-after keynote speaker and advisor on accessibility, resilience, and high performance. She helps organizations design systems that enable people to perform at their best, even in less-than-perfect circumstances.

- **Melissa Guenette**, a marketing and PR strategist who spent over two decades helping others build their brands. When she finally wrote her own book, *Start from Experience*, it transformed her visibility and confidence. Her book became a platform that opened doors to media features, new clients, speaking opportunities, and collaborations that positioned her as a thought leader; not just behind the scenes, but at the forefront of her industry.

- **Charles Achampong**, who documented his family's sabbatical year in *Around the World in Family Days*. What began as a travel story became a deeper reflection on presence, clarity, and the power of pausing. His book became his credibility passport, leading to keynote invitations, executive workshops, and meaningful conversations about resilience and leadership.

These weren't accidents. They followed the same system you're about to learn.

What Makes This System Different

Traditional publishing advice treats your book as an isolated project. Write it, publish it, hope for the best. That's backward.

Our system treats your book as an **integrated business asset** from day one. Before you write a single word, you'll know:

- Exactly who will buy your book (and your higher-ticket offers)

- How your book fits into your overall business model

- What products and services your book will naturally lead to

- How to build your audience WHILE you write

You'll also learn strategies that most authors never discover:

- How to use speaking engagements to sell your

book AND high-ticket programs

- The media outlet strategy that builds your authority while promoting your book (we've included our exact list of twenty-one outlets that accept thought leadership articles)

- The book launch event formula that can generate six figures in revenue in a single weekend

- How to leverage your book into sponsorships, partnerships, and opportunities you never imagined

Your Business Transformation Starts Here

By the time you finish this book and implement our system, you'll have:

- A published book that positions you as an expert

- A clear path from book to business growth

- A personal brand that attracts ideal clients

- Multiple income streams flowing from your expertise

- The confidence that comes from being a published author

More importantly, you'll understand something most people never grasp.

Your book is not just about sharing information. It's about building a business and a brand that creates freedom, impact, and income.

Think about where you'll be twelve months from now. Will you still be talking about "someday writing a book"? Or will you be a published author fielding opportunities, attracting dream clients, and building the business you've always wanted?

The choice is yours. The system is here. Let's begin.

Part One:
The Foundation

1
From Idea to Intention: Your Book as Business Strategy

Before you write a single word, before you even know what your book is about, you need to answer one question: Why?

Not "Why should anyone read this?" or "Why am I qualified?" Just: Why are you writing this book?

We call this your Contract With Yourself, and it's the foundation everything else builds on. Without a strong why, your book becomes another abandoned project. With it, you have an anchor that pulls you through every moment of doubt.

But here's what most writing advice won't tell you: **Your "why" should include your business goals.** In fact, it must. Because when you see your book as a business asset from the beginning, everything changes.

The Four Whys (Plus the Business Why)

Through working with hundreds of authors, we've

discovered that most people write books for one of four reasons, but successful author-entrepreneurs add a fifth dimension: the business impact.

1. The Passion Project (Legacy)

This is the book of your heart. Maybe it's your life story, lessons learned, or wisdom you want to pass down. Even if only your children and grandchildren read it, it's worth it to you. This is about leaving something behind, creating something that outlives you.

🍀
Author Spotlight – Shelley A. Murdock

When Shelley came to us with her book idea, we asked her why she wanted to write it. Her answer was simple: to leave a legacy of health, strength, and longevity for her family and for women everywhere.

In her 60s, with a beautiful life devoted to fitness and wellbeing, Shelley decided it was time to capture decades of knowledge and experience in a book that would inspire others to live with vitality at every age. Her first book, *Healthy & Fit for Life: The Starter Kit for Women Over 50*, became an international bestseller and a trusted guide for women ready to rebuild strength, energy, and confidence.

Her second book, *In Search of Longevity: How to*

Engineer a Life with Healthy Habits, also became a #1 bestseller, and it took on a life of its own. What began as a legacy project evolved into a thriving business and movement. Today, Shelley provides fitness and longevity experiences at events and conferences, leads a six-month signature coaching program that helps women engineer healthier, more energized lives, and trains clients virtually across the world.

Shelley's story shows that a book can start as a legacy and grow into something much bigger, a living, breathing expression of your purpose that continues to create impact, connection, and opportunity long after the last page is written.

That's what a Passion Project can do. It becomes both a legacy and a launchpad.

The Business Layer

Even passion projects can build businesses. Your authentic story attracts people who resonate with your journey. They don't just want to read your book, they want to learn from you, work with you, and be in your community.

2. The Shared Experience

You've been through something that changed you. Weight loss, illness, career challenges, parenting struggles. You want to help others navigate the same journey. Your book becomes a flashlight for people walking the path you've already traveled.

The Business Layer

Shared experience books naturally lead to coaching, courses, and communities. People who've overcome challenges will pay premium prices to work with someone who's been there. Your book is proof you understand their struggle.

3. Business Growth (The Direct Path)

Your book turns your business card into a billboard that never stops working. It positions you as an expert, attracts clients, and opens doors to speaking opportunities.

The Business Layer

This is the most obvious business play, but most authors still underestimate its power. Your book should be designed from the start to:

- Qualify ideal clients

- Demonstrate your methodology

- Create natural pathways to your offers

- Establish pricing authority (if you wrote THE book, you can charge premium fees)

4. The Full-Time Author Path

You see books as your business. Maybe you want to write multiple books, become a speaker, or build an empire around your writing. Your first book is the foundation of something bigger.

The Business Layer

Book income alone rarely creates wealth, but books that lead to ghostwriting services, courses, events, coaching, and speaking absolutely can. We'll show you how.

5. The Media and Opportunity Magnet (The Hidden Fifth Why)

Here's what most authors discover AFTER publishing: the

book opens doors they never expected.

Podcast hosts love interviewing authors (we've included our podcast business strategy in Chapter 8). Conference planners seek published experts as keynote speakers. Media outlets quote people who've written books. Corporate clients hire authors as consultants. Each of these opportunities pays far more than book sales ever will.

One of our authors, a mental health consultant, found that her $20 book led to:

- 50+ podcast interviews (exposure to 500,000+ potential clients)

- 12 paid speaking engagements ($5,000-$15,000 each)

- 3 corporate consulting contracts (total value: $180,000)

- A TEDx talk invitation

- Regular contributor status in national TV media

Her book investment? Under $10,000. Her return in the first year? Over $300,000.

That's the power of "Write the Book, Build the Business, Be the Brand."

Your Integrated Why Statement

Now let's create YOUR why statement that integrates personal purpose with business strategy. Fill in these prompts:

Personal Why: I'm writing this book because:

_____

This message matters now because:

_____

Business Why: This book will help me build my business by:

_____

The ideal clients I'll attract through this book are:

_____

My book will lead naturally to these offers:

- Offer 1:

_____

- Offer 2:

_____

- Offer 3:

_____

Brand Why: Being a published author will position me as:

_____

The opportunities I expect to receive because of my book:

_____

My author brand in one sentence:

_____

The 10-Minute Strategic Brain Dump

Now that you know your integrated why, let's find out what you're writing about with a business lens.

Set a timer for 10 minutes. Grab paper (not your computer, there's something powerful about pen and paper for this). Write down every book idea you could possibly write about, but THIS TIME, note the business potential next to each.

For example:

- "Teach people to make sourdough bread" → Could lead to: baking courses, kitchen tool affiliate income, subscription recipe service

- "My grandmother's immigration story" → Could lead to: legacy preservation service, family history workshops, speaking at cultural organizations

- "How to survive your first year of teaching" →

Could lead to: teacher training programs, school district consulting, education conference speaking

See the difference? You're not just listing book ideas. You're seeing them as business opportunities.

Most people stop at five or six ideas. Push past that. The gold often comes after you think you're out of ideas.

When your timer goes off, look at your list. Circle the three that make BOTH your heart beat faster AND your business brain light up.

Want our exact "Brain Dump" worksheet?
Download it here: LuckyBookPublishing.com/book

The Business-Aligned Three-Question Filter

Now filter your three ideas through our business-aligned version of the Three-Question Filter:

Question 1: Which book can I write fastest AND offers clear business applications?

You want speed to market for two reasons. First, done beats perfect. Second, the sooner your book exists, the sooner it starts working as a business development tool.

Look for the book where you:

- Already have most of the content in your head

- Can clearly see how it leads to paid offers

- Have proven methods that deliver results for clients

Question 2: Which idea will most likely result in a finished book AND attract paying clients?

Some ideas excite you but won't necessarily attract clients willing to pay. Others might have huge business potential but you'll never finish writing them. You need both.

Consider:

- Does this topic have demonstrated market demand?

- Are people already paying for solutions in this space?

- Can I prove my methodology works?

- Will this position me for higher-ticket opportunities?

Question 3: Which idea makes me happiest AND has the strongest business model?

When you imagine holding your finished book, which topic makes you smile? Which one would you be proud to hand someone at a networking event? And critically: Which one naturally leads to the business you want to build?

One of our authors chose between writing about

personal productivity (broad market, lower prices) versus executive leadership transformation (narrow market, premium prices). The productivity book might have sold more copies. But the leadership book positioned him for $25,000 consulting engagements with C-suite executives. He chose leadership. In year one, his book generated under $5,000 in direct sales but over $400,000 in consulting revenue.

Usually, one idea scores well on all three questions. That's your book.

From Book Topic to Business Model

Once you've chosen your book topic, map out the business model BEFORE you start writing:

The Business Model Canvas for Your Book:

Front-End (Your Book)

- Price point: $_____ (typically $15-30)

- Projected sales in Year 1: _____

- Total book revenue: $_____

Mid-Tier Offers (What Your Book Leads To)

- Online course: $_____ (typically $200-2,000)

- Group coaching: $_____ per person (typically $500-5,000)

- Workshop/Event ticket: $_____ (typically $300-3,000)

- Projected clients: _____

- Total mid-tier revenue: $_____

High-Tier Offers (Your Premium Services)

- VIP Day: $_____ (typically $2,500-15,000)

- Done-for-you service: $_____ (typically $5,000-50,000+)

- Private coaching: $_____ (typically $10,000-100,000+)

- Retainer/consulting: $_____ (typically $5,000-25,000/month)

- Projected clients: _____

- Total high-tier revenue: $_____

Opportunity Income (What Your Author Status Creates)

- Speaking fees: $_____ per event × _____ events = $_____

- Corporate training: $_____ per engagement × _____ engagements = $_____

- Media/content opportunities: $_____

- Affiliate/sponsor income: $_____

- Total opportunity revenue: $_____

Total Projected Annual Revenue from Your Book Ecosystem: $_____

This exercise does three powerful things:

1. **It shifts your mindset** from "I hope my book sells" to "My book is the engine of a multi-revenue-stream business"

2. **It clarifies your book's real job:** not to make money directly, but to attract ideal clients who invest in your higher-ticket offers

3. **It makes the book investment obvious:** if spending $10,000-$15,000 to publish your book can generate $100,000+ in business revenue, it's not an expense. It's your highest-ROI investment.

Real Example: From Book Topic to $500K Business

Let me show you how this worked for one of our authors, who wrote a book about overcoming burnout and leading with balance in the corporate world.

Their Why:

- **Personal:** Tired of seeing high-performing professionals burn out while chasing success.

- **Business:** Wanted to transition from a demanding corporate leadership role into coaching and consulting focused on sustainable performance.

- **Brand:** Wanted to be recognized as a trusted voice in wellbeing and leadership.

Their Business Model:

Front-End:

- Book: $20 × 2,000 copies = $40,000

Mid-Tier:

- Online course: $497 × 300 people = $149,100

- Quarterly webinars: $97 × 150 people × 4 quarters = $58,200

High-Tier:

- Corporate wellness consulting: $5,000 per session × 12 companies = $60,000

- Leadership Coaching packages: $10,000 × 8 businesses = $80,000

- Ongoing retainers: $2,000/month × 10 clients × 12 months = $240,000

Speaking/Media:

- Conference speaking: $7,500 × 4 events = $30,000

Total Year 1 Revenue: $657,300

Their book investment: $8,500

Their time investment to write: 12 weeks

Not bad for three months of focused work.

Your Commitment: Business-Focused

Before we dive into the method, you need to make a commitment. Not to us, not to some future readers, but to yourself.

I commit to:

1. **Writing this book with my business goals in mind:** Every chapter will be designed to demonstrate my expertise and lead readers toward working with me.

2. **Seeing this as a business investment**, not a vanity project, I will track my ROI and treat this book as my most valuable marketing asset.

3. **Finishing this book even if it's not perfect**: Done beats perfect because only a published book builds a business.

4. **Building while I write**: I will start attracting clients and building my audience before the book is even finished.

5. **Thinking beyond book sales**: My success metric isn't copies sold, it's business revenue generated and opportunities created.

That last point is crucial. Chasing bestseller lists is fine as a vanity metric, but it won't pay your mortgage. Building a business around your book? That creates life-changing income.

Planning your author business model?
Get the editable Book-to-Business Canvas
LuckyBookPublishing.com/book

The Next Steps: Writing with Business Intent

In the next chapter, we'll dive into the Brain Dump Method, how to get all your expertise out of your head and organized in a way that naturally leads to business opportunities.

But first, complete your integrated why statement and business model canvas. Print them out. Put them where you'll see them every day.

These aren't just planning documents. They're your roadmap from "aspiring author" to "published expert with a thriving business."

Let's do this.

Owning Her Authority

SARAH BOYD

Personal Trainer, Nutrition & Lifestyle Coach

For Sarah Boyd, writing her book was more than a professional milestone, it was a reclamation of confidence and clarity. After years of helping women transform their health and habits, she finally put her knowledge into words. The result was unexpected: even before publication, the process itself elevated her authority, strengthened her message, and deepened her belief in her work.

Partnering with Lucky Book Publishing helped Sarah lean into generosity and authenticity. *"People don't pay for information, they pay for transformation,"* Samantha and Simar reminded her. That insight freed her to write openly, to give everything she had, and to trust that her voice would resonate.

Today, Sarah's message is sparking a shift in women's wellness. Her clients are lifting heavier, eating better, and embracing strength without shame. Through her work, Sarah is redefining what it means to live healthy, proving that the power to change was always within us.

Connect with Sarah Boyd:
🌐 SarahBoyd.ca
✉ sarah@sarahboyd.ca

Re-Writing the Plan and Healing

MARIAH SCRIVENS

Business Coach, Author & Mom of Three Under Two

For Mariah Scrivens, the idea to write a book began as a business tool. a way to extend her coaching impact. But through the process, she found herself looking her past in the eye, working through decades of unprocessed experiences through the lens of her recent ADHD diagnosis. What started as content creation became healing, clarity, and a reclamation.

Partnering with Lucky Book Publishing meant more than producing a manuscript. It meant investing in herself, her story, her worth, and her excellence. "I didn't just need help writing the book," she says. "I needed someone to help me *keep showing up for it*." That support pushed her to share, to market, and to keep the conversation alive.

Today, Mariah's journey has opened unexpected doors, from connecting deeply with readers who feel seen for the first time, to stepping into new leadership as Lucky Book's Fractional CMO. What began as a strategy became a new beginning.

Connect with Mariah Scrivens:
🌐 MariahScrivens.com
✉ mariah@mariahscrivens.com

Writing the Book was Just the Beginning

Julee Sung

Career Coach, Author

For Julee Sung, writing Thrive and Shine began as an act of courage. "I never thought of myself as a writer," she says. "I thought there was a certain type of person who would be a writer. They would sound a certain way, bring certain credentials, have some kind of background that let them be writers somehow."

But that belief shifted the moment she joined the Lucky Book Publishing community. "Working with Sam and Simar and the Lucky Book family gave me that space to breathe, to ask questions, and to accept that what I had to say was actually important." Through their guidance, Julee learned that taking small action steps forward versus overthinking, was the key to overcoming fear. "All those barriers that were kind of in my way started to fall. Seeing other authors lead by example was also really inspiring."

Today, Julee's Thrive and Shine message ripples through her book, engaging workshops and one-on-one coaching programs. "Nobody knows what they're doing. So don't worry about it," she reminds readers. "You are enough and special and valuable and gifted as you are today." Her words invite early-stage professionals to embrace growth while realizing they are already thriving. "Just love yourself, be kind to yourself, and keep thriving and keep shining."

Connect with Julee Sung:
🌐 JuleeSung.com
 julees94

2

The Brain Dump Method: Mining Your Gold for Business Impact

You have more content than you think.

Every author we've worked with, from the CEO who thought she had "maybe three chapters' worth" to the teacher who worried he was "too boring," discovered they had enough material for multiple books. The challenge isn't having enough to say. It's organizing what you already know into a framework that serves your readers AND your business.

That's where the Brain Dump Method comes in.
This isn't creative writing or waiting for inspiration. It's a systematic extraction of the knowledge you already possess, structured in a way that positions you as an expert and naturally leads readers to want more from you.

The Content Mining Process

Get a fresh notebook or open a new document. At the top, write your book topic. Now, we're going to mine your brain for gold using seven specific prompts. Don't think too hard. Just write.

But here's the business twist: As you write, start noticing patterns. What you're really doing is identifying your signature methodology, your unique frameworks, your proprietary processes. These become the foundation of everything you sell.

Prompt 1: What stories do you have on this topic?

Every piece of wisdom you have came from somewhere. Maybe you learned about resilience when your first business failed. Maybe you discovered a productivity hack during your busiest year. Write down every story connected to your topic. Yours, your clients', even stories you've heard that stuck with you.

We discovered the power of stories accidentally. Our fifth author was writing about project management, spreadsheets, Gantt charts, and critical paths. A little dry, right? In our first meeting, she mentioned offhand how she'd saved a million-dollar project by using sticky notes on her living room wall when all the fancy software failed. We stopped her. "Tell us more about that."

For the next twenty minutes, she shared the whole story:

the panic when the server crashed, the team gathered in her living room at midnight, the moment when moving one sticky note revealed the problem that had stumped them for weeks.

"That," we told her, "needs to be in your book."

She resisted. "But it's not professional. It's not a proper methodology."

"It's real," we said. "It's memorable. And it teaches the principle better than any flow chart could."

That story became her chapter opener. Readers mention it more than any other part of her book. They remember the sticky notes. More importantly, they remember the lesson: Sometimes the simplest tools are the most powerful.

But here's what she discovered later: That story became her signature. In every keynote speech, every consulting pitch, every podcast interview, she tells the sticky note story. It's become her brand. And when corporate clients hire her for $15,000 consulting engagements, they say, "We need someone who thinks like that. Someone who can cut through complexity."

One story. Repeated hundreds of times. Directly responsible for hundreds of thousands in revenue.

> Your stories are not just illustrations. They're your intellectual property. They're what make YOU different from every other expert in your field.

As you write your stories, ask yourself:

- Which stories demonstrate my unique approach?

- Which ones show transformation or results?

- Which could become signature stories I tell in speeches and pitches?

- Which proves I can solve the exact problems my ideal clients face?

Samantha understands this deeply. As a teenager, she spent time volunteering at her mother's workplace, a nursing home and retirement home. She would call bingo, help with social activities, give out cookies and coffee, and sit with older people. She loved hearing their stories, making them smile, and helping people feel seen and heard. Those experiences taught her that stories are how we connect, how we share wisdom, how we make impact real and personal.

Stories are the carrier waves for information. People forget facts but remember stories. One of our authors was writing about financial planning. Boring at first, right? But when she shared the story of her dad's peaceful last years because he'd planned well versus her uncle's stressful situation, suddenly financial planning became deeply emotional and memorable. That contrast story now appears in all her marketing materials and is the opening to her $5,000 financial planning workshop.

Prompt 2: What are the main ideas and key concepts?

If you had to teach a masterclass on your topic, what would be your main points? Don't worry about the order yet. Just list them. These become the backbone of your chapters, and your signature methodology.

When Simar did this exercise for our first book about publishing, she thought she had maybe five main concepts. She set a timer for ten minutes and started writing. Twenty-three ideas later, she was still going. Not all of them became chapters, but they all became content. Some became subsections, some became social media posts, some became bonuses for our course. Nothing is wasted when you mine your knowledge systematically.

Here's the business strategy: As you list your main concepts, you're actually building your curriculum. These same concepts become:

- Chapter topics in your book

- Module topics in your course

- Session topics in your group coaching program

- Workshop sections in your corporate training

- Pillar content for your social media

- Newsletter themes

- Podcast episode topics

One framework. Multiple revenue streams.

Look at what you've written. Can you organize these concepts into a 3-5 step process? A framework? A system? If so, name it. Seriously. Give it a name.

Examples:

- "The Sticky Note Strategy" (project management)

- "The 5 Pillars of Purpose-Driven Profit" (business strategy)

- "The Freedom Family Formula" (work-life integration)

- "The Confident Speaker System" (presentation skills)

Why name it? Because named frameworks are:

- Easy to trademark

- Simple to reference and teach

- Memorable for clients

- Perceived as more valuable

- The foundation of premium offers

One of our authors created "The Clarity Cascade," a 4-step process for decision-making. That framework appears in her $20 book, her $2,000 course, and her $25,000 consulting engagements. Same framework, different price points, different implementation levels. Her book explains WHAT the framework is. Her course teaches HOW to implement it yourself. Her consulting does it WITH you and FOR you.

That's how you build a business, not just write a book.

Prompt 3: What examples and real-life experiences can you share?

Theory is important, but examples make it real. What have you seen work? What have you seen fail? What case studies can you share? Even if you need to anonymize them, these real-world applications are gold.

We learned this from author number twenty-two, a consultant who'd been helping companies improve their culture for fifteen years. Her first draft was all theory: definitions, frameworks, models. Technically correct but impossibly boring. We pushed her: "Tell us about a real company you helped."

"I can't," she said. "Confidentiality."

"Then change the details. Make it a composite. But make it real."

She came back with a story about "TechCo" (not its real name), a startup where employees were quitting faster than they could hire. She described the CEO who thought ping pong tables would fix morale while ignoring that people were working sixteen-hour days. She shared the conversation that changed everything, the small shifts that created big results, the email from an employee six months later saying it was the first time in two years they'd had dinner with their family.

That chapter went from academic to unforgettable. Readers could see themselves in the story. More importantly, they could see the path forward.

But here's what happened next: That TechCo case study became the centerpiece of her sales conversations. When potential corporate clients asked, "Can you really change culture?" she'd tell that story. Her close rate went from 30% to 80%. Why? Because the story provided proof without being salesy. It showed transformation, not theory.

Your examples serve double duty: They make your book compelling AND they provide social proof for your services.

As you document your examples, create a "Results Bank."

Results Bank Examples

- Client transformations (with specific metrics when possible)
- Before-and-after scenarios
- Common mistakes and how you fixed them
- Surprising discoveries and breakthroughs

This Results Bank becomes sales material for everything you offer.

Prompt 4: What are the lessons learned?

Every experience teaches something. What did you learn the hard way that you can help others avoid? What did you discover that surprised you? These lessons become the "aha moments" your readers will remember, and the insights that make them think, "I need to work with this person."

Think about the mistakes you made before you figured out your approach. Those mistakes are valuable because your readers are probably making them right now. When you say, "I used to think X, but I learned Y," readers think, "That's exactly where I am! If they got through this, maybe I can too."

One of our authors, a nutritionist, built her entire book

around the twelve diet mistakes she made before finding her approach. Each chapter: one mistake, what it cost her, what she learned, the better approach. Simple structure. Powerful impact. And guess what? Her most expensive coaching package is called "The 12-Week Transformation" – one week per lesson from her book. Her book is literally the curriculum for her $10,000 coaching program.

Prompt 5: What are the broken record conversations you've had on this topic?

You know those conversations you have over and over? The advice you find yourself giving repeatedly? The questions people always ask you? That's book content. If multiple people need to hear it, many more will benefit from reading it.

We discovered this ourselves. Simar kept having the same conversation with aspiring authors about title creation. Same questions, same answers, over and over. That became our entire chapter on "Clear Not Clever" titles. Your broken record conversations are telling you what people need to know.

Business insight: These repeated conversations are also telling you what your signature talk should be about, what your lead magnet should address, what workshop you should offer. The topics that come up repeatedly are the topics with proven market demand.

Make a List Right Now

- What do people always ask me about?
- What advice do I give most often?
- What misconceptions do I constantly correct?
- What simple thing do I know that others struggle with?

These questions reveal gaps in the market, problems that need solutions. Problems people will pay to solve.

Prompt 6: What other books have you read that sparked ideas?

You don't write in a vacuum. What books influenced your thinking? What did they miss that you can add? What did they get wrong that you can correct? What did they explain in a complex way that you can simplify?

This isn't about copying. It's about joining a conversation. Every book builds on what came before. Yours will too.

Strategic approach: If you can position your book as "the next step" after a popular book in your field, you inherit that book's audience. In your marketing, you can say: "If you loved [Popular Book], you'll want to read [Your Book] because it shows you how to actually implement those ideas."

One of our authors wrote a book about productivity for creative people. In her introduction, she wrote: "If you've read *Getting Things Done* and thought 'That's great for linear thinkers, but my brain doesn't work that way,' this book is for you." Brilliant positioning. She wasn't competing with GTD, she was complementing it and capturing the people it didn't serve.

Prompt 7: What are the key takeaway messages?

If readers remember only three things from your book, what should they be? These become your through-lines, the messages you'll weave throughout your chapters.

But think bigger: **These key messages also become your brand pillars.**

For example, our key messages are:

1. Writing a book isn't about talent; it's about having the right method.

2. Your book is a business asset, not just a creative project.

3. Done beats perfect. A published book builds businesses, but a perfect unpublished book helps no one.

These three messages appear in:

- Every chapter of our book

- Our website copy

- Our social media content

- Our client onboarding

- Our podcast interviews

- Our speaking engagements

When people think of us, they think of these messages. That's brand consistency. And brand consistency builds trust. And trust generates revenue.

Real Interview Insights: What Authors Wish They'd Known

Let's look at what real authors told us about their book journey. These insights come from our community survey:

On finding their book topic:

One author shared: "I thought I needed to write the most comprehensive guide ever written on my topic. That paralyzing ambition kept me stuck for two years. When I finally just focused on solving ONE specific problem for ONE specific person, the book practically wrote itself."

Another said: "My book topic emerged from paying attention to what people kept asking me about. I didn't need to invent a new idea, I just needed to document what I was already doing."

On the business impact:

"Within three months of publishing, I had podcast invitations, speaking requests, and client inquiries. The book acted like a 24/7 salesperson working on my behalf." – Marketing consultant

"I raised my prices 40% after publishing my book. Not because my services changed, but because my perceived authority changed. The book gave me permission to charge what I'm worth." – Business coach

"My book replaced five years of content marketing. Instead of proving my expertise with hundreds of blog posts, I could just say 'I wrote the book on this' because I literally did." – Technology consultant

On the writing process:

"I wish I'd known that my first draft didn't need to be perfect. I wasted months polishing chapter one when I should have been writing chapters two through ten." – Health coach

"The brain dump method saved me. Once I stopped trying to 'write' and just started documenting what I already knew, everything flowed." – Real estate investor

These are real insights from real authors who've walked this path. Learn from them. Skip the mistakes they made. Use the strategies that worked for them.

The Organization System

Now you have pages of raw material. Time to organize it into chapters. This is where most people get stuck, but we have a simple system that works.

First, look at everything you've written. You'll notice natural patterns. Maybe several stories are about overcoming fear. Maybe multiple concepts relate to planning. These groupings are telling you what your chapters are.

Take sticky notes or index cards. Write one main idea on each. Spread them out on a table or floor. Start grouping related ideas together. Don't force it, let the natural connections emerge.

Most non-fiction books have 7-10 chapters. Each chapter covers one main concept with multiple supporting points. If you have twenty groupings, you're either looking at multiple books or you need to combine some groups.

Here's our chapter structure that works for any non-fiction book, and naturally leads to business opportunities:

Chapter Opening:

- Hook (story, surprising fact, or question)

- What this chapter will cover (1-3 sentences)

- Why it matters to the reader, AND why it matters

for their business/success

- How this chapter builds on the previous one

Chapter Body:

- Main concept explained

- Your unique framework or approach (this is what makes you different)

- 2-3 supporting stories or examples

- Practical application

- Common mistakes to avoid

- What this looks like when done right vs. done wrong

Chapter Closing:

- 5-10 bullet point summary

- 3-5 reflection questions for the reader

- One action step they can take immediately

- How this chapter connects to what's next

Business Integration Points (woven throughout, not separate):

- At least one example of how this concept applies in business/professional settings

- One "level up" mention. Hint at deeper

implementation available through your services

- One client success story (even if anonymized) showing real-world results

This structure does multiple things. It respects different learning styles (some people want summaries, others want stories). It makes your book skimmable for busy readers. And it turns passive reading into active engagement.

But most importantly, it positions you as someone who doesn't just share information, you provide transformation. That's what people pay for.

The 30,000 Word Sweet Spot (And What Each Section Sells)

Most successful non-fiction books are around 30,000 words. That's about 120 pages. It's long enough to deliver value, short enough to keep attention, and perfect for establishing authority without overwhelming readers.

That said, 30,000 words is an industry benchmark, not a rule. Your book can be shorter and still be wildly effective, as long as it's paired with the right business strategy. A powerful 15,000-20,000 word book, when connected to your offer, your message, and your brand ecosystem, can build just as much impact, authority, and income. The key is strategy and clarity, not word count.

Here's the breakdown using the 30k wordcount example; with the business strategy for each section:

Book Outline – A Snapshot

Introduction: 2,000 words

- Purpose: Hook readers and establish credibility

- Business strategy: Position your unique approach, hint at the transformation possible

- What it sells: Your worldview and authority

8 Chapters: 3,500 words each (28,000 words)

- Purpose: Deliver your core methodology

- Business strategy: Each chapter demonstrates one aspect of your signature system

- What it sells: Your framework and expertise

Conclusion: 1,500 words

- Purpose: Inspire action and provide next steps

- Business strategy: Clear path to continued relationship (course, coaching, community)

- What it sells: The next level of implementation with your guidance

Additional elements: 500 words

- Acknowledgments: Build community and gratitude

- Resources: Add value and position you as a connector

- About the Author: Reinforce authority and provide contact info

- What it sells: Your personality and accessibility

Total: About 32,000 words

That's roughly 7-8 pages per chapter. Completely doable.

If you're thinking "I could never write that much," remember: You just brain dumped probably 2,000 words in 30 minutes. You have more content than you think.

And if you're thinking "That's not enough for everything I want to say," perfect, you've got book two waiting. Or better yet, you've got a comprehensive course or coaching program that goes deeper than the book ever could. Remember: Your book is the gateway, not the destination.

The Expansion Technique (That Builds Your Entire Content Library)

For each chapter, repeat the brain dump process. If Chapter 3 is about "Building Resilience," do a focused brain dump just on resilience. What stories do you have about that specific topic? What are the key concepts within resilience?

This recursive process means you never face a blank page. You're always working from material you've already generated. Writer's block becomes impossible because you're not creating from nothing, you're organizing what you already know.

The Business Multiplier

Every time you do this deep dive on a chapter topic, you're actually creating content for multiple formats.

That "Building Resilience" chapter expansion might generate:

- 3,500 words for your book chapter

- 5 blog posts (700 words each)

- 10 social media posts

- 3 video scripts

- 1 webinar outline

- 1 podcast episode outline

- 5 email newsletter topics

- Workshop material for a 2-hour training session

- Module content for an online course

One expansion session. Dozens of content pieces. All reinforcing your expertise. All pointing back to your book and your services.

One author came to us convinced she had "maybe 10 pages of content." Using this method, she wrote a 35,000-word book in six weeks. She didn't learn anything new or become more creative. She just systematically extracted what was already in her head.

Then she took those chapter expansions and created a 6-week course that sold for $1,997. Same content, deeper implementation, higher price point. Her book was the marketing for the course. The course was the implementation of the book. Both made money. Both built her business.

From Brain Dump to Business Blueprint

Before we move to the next chapter, let's make this concrete. Here's your assignment:

Part 1: Complete Your Brain Dumps

- Spend 10 minutes on each of the seven prompts
- Don't edit, just extract
- Look for patterns and groupings
- Identify your potential signature framework

Part 2: Map Your Business Model

For each major concept/chapter topic you've identified, fill this out:

Chapter Topic: _____

What this chapter teaches: _____

The results readers can expect:

_____

The deeper implementation I could offer:

- DIY option (course/program): $_____

- Done-with-you option (group coaching): $_____

- Done-for-you option (private coaching/consulting): $_____

How I'll hint at these options in the chapter:

_____

Part 3: Create Your Content Multiplication Plan

Choose your three strongest chapter topics. For each:

- List 5 social media posts you could create

- Outline 1 lead magnet (free download)

- Sketch 1 workshop or webinar

- Describe 1 deeper-dive paid offer

See what you're doing? You're not just writing a book. You're building a content ecosystem and business infrastructure. Your book is the hub. Everything else radiates from it.

This is what "Write the Book, Build the Business, Be the Brand" looks like in practice.

The Mindset Shift: From Author to Authority

One final mindset shift before we move on: Stop thinking of yourself as "someone who's writing a book" and start thinking of yourself as "an authority who's documenting their expertise."

The first mindset creates anxiety. "Am I good enough? Is my writing good enough? Will anyone care?"

The second creates confidence. "I've solved these problems dozens of times. I'm simply sharing what I know. People need this information."

Your book isn't creative fiction where you're making things up. It's business non-fiction where you're organizing knowledge you already have. You're not an aspiring author hoping for validation. You're an expert creating a tool that will serve your readers and grow your business.

That's the truth. Own it.

The Force Within: Showing Up Fully and Living Your Truth

CONNIE ROTELLA

CEO, Arts Industry Leader, Author

For Connie Rotella, writing *The Force Within* was more than a creative project, it was a calling. Each chapter became a lesson in presence, reminding her that every step of the journey counts. From learning the tools to express what her heart wanted to say, to connecting with readers in honest, heartfelt conversations, Connie discovered the deeper reason this book was meant to come through her.

Partnering with Lucky Book Publishing helped her turn inspiration into impact. The process opened doors to new opportunities, from speaking engagements to community events, allowing her to share her message of truth, connection, and growth with wider audiences.

Today, *The Force Within* continues to spark meaningful dialogue and remind readers of the power in showing up authentically. Connie's message is both simple and profound: *Show up to your life and watch what unfolds when you do.*

Connect with Connie Rotella:
🌐 ConnieRotella.com
✉ info@connierotella.com

Channeling Purpose into a Movement of Self-Awareness

ELLIE LALIBERTÉ

Award Winning Author, Book and Self-Awareness Coach

When Ellie Laliberté began writing *Letters From You to You*, she was in a moment of complete surrender. Her Airbnb management business had reached its end, and she opened her laptop with no plan, only a willingness to receive what needed to be written. Within a month, the words poured through her, transforming both her identity and her direction.

Partnering with Lucky Book Publishing turned that intuitive creation into a global ripple. Ellie's book, recognized internationally for its creativity, has touched hundreds of hearts and led her into her next calling, as an award-winning author and Book Coach guiding others to find their voice. With Lucky Book's support, she discovered her own marketing power, building her website, crafting reels, and sharing her message on podcasts worldwide.

Ellie now helps others channel their truth through the written word, proving that when you trust the process, the book doesn't just change your life, it shows you who you're meant to become.

Connect with Ellie Laliberté:
🌐 LettersByEllie.com
✉ info@lettersbyellie.com

3

The Customer Research Secret: Writing for Real Readers Who Become Real Clients

---

Here's where most writing advice gets it wrong. They tell you to "write for yourself" or "write what you know." But a book that changes everything isn't written for you, it's written for a specific reader who needs what you have to offer.

And here's the business truth that changes everything:

The better you understand your reader,
the better you can serve them.
The better you serve them,
the more they'll want to work with you.

This is where our Customer Research process comes in. It's the difference between a book that sits on a shelf and one that spreads like wildfire and generates serious business revenue.

The Avatar Creation Process (That Doubles as Client Research)

You're going to create a detailed portrait of your ideal reader. Not "women aged 35-55" or "entrepreneurs." We mean a specific person so real you could pick them out of a crowd.

We learned this the hard way. Our early authors would say their book was "for everyone who wants to improve their life." These books struggled. Then we started forcing specificity, and magic happened. Books found their audiences. Readers said, "It's like this was written just for me." And those readers became clients, community members, and raving fans.

Answer these ten questions about your ideal reader and notice how this process is identical to identifying your ideal client:

1. What is their gender? Be specific. This doesn't mean others won't read your book, but you need to picture someone specific while writing. If you're writing about entrepreneurship, does your reader identify as male, female, non-binary? The language you use, the examples you choose, the pain points you address all shift based on this answer.

2. What is their exact age? Not a range. Pick an age.

Simar pictures a 29-year-old entrepreneur. Samantha pictures a 42-year-old professional woman. That specificity changes everything from language to examples to cultural references.

A 29-year-old talks about "building my dream business." A 42-year-old talks about "finally doing what I was meant to do." Same desire, different language. Get this right and your reader thinks, "You get me."

3. What is their relationship status? Do they have kids? A single 25-year-old has different concerns than a married parent of three. Know who you're talking to.

Your reader's life situation affects:

- How much time they have (busy parents need quick wins)

- What they're worried about (supporting a family vs. personal freedom)

- What they can invest (both time and money)

- What success looks like to them

One of our authors made a critical pivot when she realized her ideal reader was a mom with young kids, not a single professional. Her entire book shifted from "build your empire" to "build your business around your family." That specificity made her the go-to expert for mom entrepreneurs, and her coaching program filled immediately because moms felt finally seen and understood.

4. What do they do for a living and how much do they make? This affects everything from the price point of your book to the examples you use. Don't talk about hiring virtual assistants if your reader makes $30,000 a year. Don't suggest budget strategies if they make $300,000.

Business critical: This answer tells you what they can invest in your services. If your ideal reader makes $250,000+, your $25,000 consulting package is accessible. If they make $50,000, you might need group coaching at $5,000. Neither is wrong, but you need to know which you're targeting.

5. What hobbies do they have? This tells you their interests, their values, where they spend their time. It helps you choose metaphors and stories that resonate.

If your reader loves running marathons, you can talk about "hitting the wall" and "finding your pace" and "training for the long game." If they love cooking, you can use kitchen analogies. These small touches make readers feel connected to you.

6. Do they have their own language? Every group has inside jokes, common phrases, shared references. Speaking their language creates instant connection.

Corporate executives talk about "moving the needle" and "getting buy-in." Coaches talk about "holding space" and "limiting beliefs." Marketers talk about "funnels" and "conversion rates." Use their language (authentically) and they recognize you as one of them.

7. What keeps them up at night? This is crucial. What worry plays on repeat in their mind at 2 AM? Your book should address this directly.

And your business offers? They're the solution to this 2 AM worry.

Examples:

- "What if I fail and prove everyone right who said I couldn't do this?"

- "What if I'm working this hard and still can't provide for my family?"

- "What if I've wasted years on the wrong path?"

- "What if I'm not enough?"

These deep fears drive purchasing decisions. When you speak to them in your book, your reader feels understood. When your coaching program promises to solve them, your reader invests.

8. What are their top 3 daily frustrations? Small, repeated frustrations often matter more than big problems. If you can solve what annoys them every single day, you become invaluable.

Examples:

- "I never have time to work ON my business, only IN it."

- "I know what to do but I can't make myself do it consistently."

- "Every time I try to grow, something breaks in my existing business."

- Your book addresses these frustrations. Your services solve them completely.

9. What does their desired situation look like? Paint the picture of where they want to be. Your book is the bridge from where they are to where they want to go.

Be specific:

- Not "I want to be successful" but "I want to wake up excited about my work, make $200K/year, and have dinner with my family every night by 6 PM."

- Not "I want to be happy" but "I want to feel confident in my decisions, proud of what I'm building, and free from constant financial stress."

The more specific the desired outcome, the more clearly you can position your book, and your services, as the path to get there.

10. What goal are they trying to achieve when they buy your book? Be specific. Not "be happier" but "stop yelling at my kids every morning." Not "make more money" but "earn enough to quit my soul-crushing job."

This is your book's promise. And your business's promise.

Would you like a template for this exercise?
Get it at LuckyBookPublishing.com/book

The Two-Avatar Strategy (That Expands Your Market)

Here's something we discovered: Most successful books speak to two avatars, not one. Often it's the same person at different life stages.

One of our authors wrote about career transition. Her two avatars were:

Avatar 1: Olivia, 26

- Early career marketing coordinator at a mid-size company

- Makes $45,000

- Feels trapped in her first "real" job

- Wants to pursue her passion (graphic design) but scared of disappointing her parents who expect her to climb the corporate ladder

- Keeps reading articles about "following your dreams" but has student loans to pay

- Single, rents an apartment with roommates

- Spends weekends on side projects but feels guilty for not working on "career building"

- 2 AM worry: "What if I'm too scared to ever make a change and wake up at 50 having wasted my life in a job I hate?"

Avatar 2: Marcus, 51

- Director of Operations at a manufacturing company

- Makes $180,000

- Successful by external measures but feels unfulfilled

- Wants to pursue meaning in his remaining career years (maybe teaching, consulting, or starting a small business)

- Has mortgage, kids in college, retirement to think about

- Married 25 years, wife is supportive but worried about financial stability

- Spends Sunday nights dreading Monday mornings

- 2 AM worry: "Is this all there is? Can I afford to make a change at my age? What if I regret not trying?"

Same topic (career transition), different life stages, slightly different approaches. But the core message, you can successfully change careers, spoke to both.

The book addressed both: Early chapters on "knowing when it's time to move" resonated with both. Middle chapters split: some addressed "transitioning early" (for Olivia), others addressed "mid-career pivots" (for Marcus). All chapters worked for both, just with different emphasis.

Result? The book appealed to a wider audience than if she'd picked just one avatar. And her business served both: She offered a $2,000 group program for early-career changers and a $15,000 VIP consulting package for executives. Same expertise, different price points, both profitable.

Creating two avatars prevents your book from being too narrow while keeping it focused. It's the sweet spot between "for everyone" and "for just this tiny group."

The Research Deep Dive (That Costs Nothing But Pays Everything)

Now comes the part that separates good books from great ones: actual research.

Go where your avatars hang out online. Facebook groups, Reddit communities, YouTube comments,

Amazon reviews of similar books. Don't post anything yet. Just read. What language do they use? What questions do they ask repeatedly? What solutions have they tried that didn't work?

We discovered this approach through failure. Our first attempt at helping authors with customer research involved surveys. "Send out a survey," we advised. "Ask people what they want." The responses were generic, unhelpful, and worst of all, dishonest. People told us what they thought we wanted to hear, not what they actually struggled with.

Then Samantha had an insight while scrolling through a Facebook group for new moms at 2 AM (she was researching for an author, not a new mom herself, but the 2 AM part was accurate, we were still figuring out work-life balance). She noticed that the questions people asked at 2 AM were different from the ones they asked at 2 PM. The 2 AM questions were raw, desperate, real. "Why won't my baby sleep?" became "I'm failing as a mother because I can't get my baby to sleep and I'm so tired I want to cry."

That's when we realized:

Don't ask people what they want.
Watch what they actually ask for when they think no one is watching.

Copy and paste the exact language they use. These become chapter titles, section headers, and marketing copy. When someone sees their exact question as your chapter title, they think, "This person gets me."

We watched one author's book take off because she used a phrase she found in a Facebook group: "Sunday Scaries." It perfectly captured the anxiety her readers felt about Monday morning. She didn't invent the phrase, she listened for it. Her book's subtitle became *Beating the Sunday Scaries: How to Love Your Work Again.* Instant connection.

The Research Deep Dive: What to Look For

The research goes deeper than just language. You're looking for patterns:

What solutions have they already tried that didn't work?

Your book needs to address why those failed. This positions you as someone who understands what they've been through. And your premium services? They're positioned as "what actually works" after everything else failed.

Example: If your avatars keep saying "I've tried meal planning but I can never stick to it," your book needs a chapter on "Why Traditional Meal Planning Fails (And What Works Instead)." Your meal planning service isn't just convenient, it's the solution after everything else failed.

What are they convinced is true that might be holding them back?

Your book needs to gently challenge these beliefs. This demonstrates thought leadership and positions you as someone who thinks differently.

Example: If everyone in your target market believes "You have to post on social media every day to grow your business," and you've discovered that's not true, that belief-busting insight becomes a key differentiator for you.

What success stories do they celebrate?

Your book needs to make these feel achievable. Show the path. Demystify the process. Make success seem possible.

Example: When you see people celebrating "I finally landed my first client!" or "I made my first $10K month!", those are the milestones your avatars care about. Your book should show how to reach them. Your coaching should guarantee reaching them faster.

What do they complain about repeatedly?

Your book needs to validate and solve these frustrations. Your paid services solve them completely.

Example: If your target market constantly complains

"I don't have time to [important thing]," your book addresses this directly. And your done-for-you service? It solves the time problem completely.

Real Research Example

One of our authors, writing about productivity for creative entrepreneurs, spent three months lurking in five Facebook groups before writing a single word. She created a document with hundreds of quotes, questions, and complaints.

Here's what she found:

Common language:

- "I'm blocked" (not "I have writer's block")

- "I can't brain today" (not "I'm tired")

- "Shoulds and have-tos" (not "obligations")

- "Shiny object syndrome" (self-aware about distraction)

Repeated frustrations:

- "I have so many ideas but can't finish anything."

- "I know what to do but I can't make myself do it."

- "Every productivity system feels too rigid for creative work."

- "I feel guilty when I'm not producing."

Failed solutions:

- Traditional time-blocking ("doesn't work for creative flow")

- Strict routines ("I rebel against my own schedules")

- "Just do it" advice ("Doesn't address WHY I'm stuck")

What they want:

- Permission to work in their own rhythm

- Systems that flex with creative energy

- Community of people who understand

- Proof that "messy" creative people can also be productive

She took all of this and:

- Used their language throughout her book (chapter title: "Shiny Object Syndrome Is Not Your Enemy")

- Addressed why traditional productivity advice fails creative people (positioning her approach as different)

- Shared stories of "messy" creatives who became productive (making success feel achievable)

- Created a system that honored creative energy rather than fighting it (her unique framework)

The result?

Her book resonated so deeply that readers felt "seen." They bought her book, joined her course, and hired her for coaching because she clearly understood them in a way no other productivity expert did.

Her research investment: Three months of lurking (cost: $0)
Her book sales in year one: $12,000
Her course sales: $180,000
Her coaching clients: $240,000
Total: $432,000

And it all started with listening.

The Validation Process (That Saves You From Wasting Time)

Before you write 30,000 words, validate that people want what you're offering. This isn't about confidence, it's about strategy.

We learned this lesson at great cost. Author number nine spent six months writing a comprehensive guide to starting a food truck business. Beautiful book. Detailed, thorough, expertly written. One problem: Her target audience wanted to know how to start a food delivery service, not a food truck. Similar but crucially different. Six months of work that missed the mark because we didn't validate first.

Now we insist on validation, and we've developed a process that takes the guesswork out of it.

Smoke Test

Create what we call a "smoke test."
Write a one-page description of your book. Include:

- The problem it solves
- Who it's for (using your avatar language)
- Three things they'll learn
- The unique approach or framework
- The result they'll achieve

Share this in relevant online communities with a soft approach: "I'm thinking about writing a book on [topic]. Is this something that would interest you? What would you want to make sure I include?"

The key is the soft approach. You're not selling, you're researching. You're not promoting, you're asking for help. People love to help, especially when you're genuinely listening.

The responses tell you everything:

If people say, "When can I buy it?" → you're on track

If they say, "That's nice" → you need to refine

If they suggest major changes → listen carefully

If they ask questions → those questions become chapter content

One author discovered through this process that everyone wanted to know about the financial side of her topic, something she'd planned to skip entirely. She thought people wanted inspiration and motivation around career change. They did, but what they really wanted was to know how to financially survive the transition. That became her most popular chapter and the foundation of her $7,500 "Financial Bridge" consulting package.

Another author thought his book about leadership was for middle managers. The validation process revealed his real audience was individual contributors who wanted to lead without formal authority. Same topic, completely different angle, and it made all the difference in how the book was received, and who hired him for consulting afterward.

Writing to One Person (Who Represents Many)

When you sit down to write, don't think about thousands of readers. Think about your one avatar. Write as if you're having coffee with them, answering their specific questions, addressing their specific fears.

Use "you" constantly. "You might be thinking…" "You've

probably experienced…" "Here's what you need to know…"

This creates what we call invisible intimacy. The reader feels like you're speaking directly to them because, in a way, you are. And when they feel understood, they want more from you. They join your email list. They follow you on social media. They buy your course. They hire you.

One of our authors gets emails constantly that say, "I felt like you were in my head! How did you know exactly what I was struggling with?" The answer? Deep avatar research. She knew because she listened.

The Empathy Bridge (That Turns Readers Into Clients)

Your reader is at Point A. Your book takes them to Point B. But here's what most authors miss: **You need to start at Point A with them.**

Don't write from where you are now, with all your knowledge and experience. Write from where you were when you were at their Point A. Remember what it felt like not to know what you know now. Remember the confusion, the overwhelm, the mistakes.

This is why personal stories matter, even in a method-focused book. When you share your Point A moment – your struggle, your confusion, your breakthrough – readers think, "If they could do it, maybe I can too."

We still remember our Point A moment vividly. Staring at the publishing industry, seeing brilliant people with important messages unable to share them, thinking, "There has to be a better way." That frustration led to Lucky Book Publishing. And that story is in our marketing, our book, and our conversations with prospective clients because it shows we've been where they are.

Your Point A story is the bridge that
helps readers believe
Point B is possible for them too.

And here's the business truth: When readers believe you understand their Point A because you've been there, they trust you to guide them to Point B. That trust converts to clients.

Map this out:

My Point A: Where I was before I figured this out

- What I was struggling with

- What I'd tried that hadn't worked

- How I felt (frustrated, confused, hopeless?)

- The moment I knew something had to change

My Journey: How I got from A to B

- The insight that changed everything

- The first step I took

- The obstacles I overcame

- The system I developed

My Point B: Where I am now

- The transformation I've experienced

- The results I've achieved

- What's possible now that wasn't before

- The business/life/freedom I have

Their Journey: How I help others get from A to B

- The book (introduction to the path)

- The course (guided implementation)

- The coaching (personalized support)

- The done-for-you (complete solution)

See how that works? Your personal journey from A to B establishes credibility and connection. Your offers are simply helping others make that same journey at different levels of support.

The Business Integration: Research That Serves Multiple Purposes

Everything we've covered in this chapter: avatar creation, language research, validation testing, serves double duty. It helps you write a better book AND build a better business.

That avatar description? Use it to:

- Guide your book writing
- Create marketing copy for your services
- Identify where to find clients
- Design your ideal client filter
- Train your team on who you serve

That language research? Use it to:

- Write compelling chapter titles
- Create social media content that resonates
- Design lead magnets that convert
- Write sales copy that connects
- Speak in a way that builds instant rapport

That validation testing? Use it to:

- Confirm market demand for your book
- Identify market demand for your services

- Build an audience before you launch

- Create buzz and anticipation

- Gather testimonials and endorsements

Nothing is wasted. Every piece of research serves your book, your business, and your brand.

Your Assignment

Before moving to Part 2 in this book, complete these tasks:

1. Create Your Detailed Avatar(s): Answer all 10 questions for at least one avatar (two if you're using the two-avatar strategy). Make them so specific you could pick them out of a crowd.

2. Do Your Research Deep Dive

- Join 3-5 online communities where your avatars hang out

- Spend at least 5 hours reading (not posting) over the next week

- Copy-paste at least 50 specific quotes, questions, or comments

- Identify patterns in language, frustrations, and desires

3. Create Your Validation Test: Write your one-page book description and share it in 2-3 communities. Collect feedback. Adjust your approach based on what you learn.

4. Map Your Empathy Bridge: Document your own Point A to Point B journey. This becomes content for your book introduction and your sales conversations.

This research phase might feel like it's delaying your writing, but it's actually accelerating it. Authors who skip this step write books that don't connect. Authors who do this work write books that build businesses.

Which would you rather have?

Want more support on your author journey?
Book a discovery call with our team at
LuckyBookPublishing.com/work-with-us

Black Girls are Already Enough

LYRIQUE RICHARDS

Author, Speaker, Confidence Coach

"I wrote this for the Black woman who's been strong for too long," she shared, her voice steady yet tender. "For the girl who learned to hide her pain just to survive."

Writing her book was both cathartic and challenging. "I had to sit with my truth and it wasn't always pretty," Lyrique admitted. "But I realized that I couldn't claim my power if my hands were full of pain." Through vulnerability, she found clarity. And through her partnership with Lucky Book Publishing, she found the confidence to share her story out loud. The process gave her community, accountability, and the belief that her words had the power to restore others.

Today, *Dear Black Girl, Let Me Hold Your Pain* stands as a testimony, a gift and a letter to every woman navigating her way through self-doubt, silence, and strength. Lyrique's message resonates far beyond the pages: "You are not broken; you are becoming." With her signature blend of raw honesty and poetic grace, she invites readers to release what no longer serves them, to stand unapologetically in their truth, and to embrace the beauty of beginning again.

Connect with Lyrique Richards:
🌐 LyriqueRichards.ca
📷 @lyrique_richards

Prevention Over Prescription

DR. KWADWO KYEREMANTENG

Physician, Author, Speaker

For Dr. Kwadwo Kyeremanteng, writing Prevention Over Prescription wasn't just about health, it was about hope. He wanted to empower people to take control of their own well-being through nutrition, movement, and community.

"It's allowed me to dream bigger," Dr. Kyeremanteng shares. "I never thought producing a book like this could reach so many people and affect so many lives."

Through his partnership with Lucky Book Publishing, he found new ways to amplify his message. "Working with them has opened doors. More speaking engagements, media requests, and collaborations. It's been a game changer."

The book's structure, infused with personal stories and quotes, became a defining element. "That one change drew people in and connected them to the heart of the message," he explains.

Since its release, Prevention Over Prescription has become a catalyst for conversation and change. Dr. Kyeremanteng now shares his insights on health and wellness through radio, podcasts, and community outreach. "I know this work makes a difference," he says. "And that's what keeps me going."

Connect with Dr. Kwadwo Kyeremanteng:
🌐 drkwadwo.ca
📷 @kwadcast

Turning Lived Experience into a Movement

JULIA DHARMA LONG

BBA, LL.B, CWMF, ANF

When Julia Dharma Long began writing *Duty to Self: A First Responder's Handbook for Building Resilience*, she carried a mission larger than a manuscript. As CEO of FRY Canada and an advocate for trauma-exposed professionals, her question was simple: *How can we equip those who protect others to also protect themselves?*

Partnering with Lucky Book Publishing gave Julia the structure and momentum to turn intention into action. Our strategic process helped her "download her brain" into a clear, compassionate framework. Together, they built more than a book; they built a movement, reframing self-care as a professional responsibility rather than a personal luxury.

Even before publication, *Duty to Self* created ripples. Julia has become a sought-after speaker and thought leader, guiding conversations around burnout, resilience, and psychological agility.

Connect with Julia Dharma Long:
🌐 FRYCanada.com | FRY-USA.com
✉ info@FRYCanada.com

Part Two:
The System

4

The Outline That Writes Itself

Every writer's nightmare: The blank page. Every writer's salvation: A detailed outline that makes the blank page impossible.

Our outline system isn't just a list of chapters. It's a complete blueprint that makes writing feel less like creating and more like assembling. You've already done the hard work in your brain dumps. Now we're going to organize that content into a structure so clear, so detailed, that the book practically writes itself.

And here's the business angle: **A well-structured book mirrors the structure of your signature program.** Your chapters become modules. Your book becomes your curriculum. Everything connects.

The Universal Book Structure

After analyzing hundreds of successful non-fiction books, we've identified a structure that works for any topic. It's not a rigid formula, it's a flexible framework that ensures your book delivers value while maintaining reader engagement.

Here's the complete structure:

Front Matter:

- Copyright Page

- Dedication (optional, but powerful for connection)

- Advance Praise (10-12 testimonials that build credibility)

- Inspiring Quote (sets the tone)

- Lead Generation Page (your freebie offer, this is crucial)

Core Content:

- Acknowledgments (build community and show gratitude)

- Preface or Author's Note (your "why" letter to readers)

- Introduction (the promise and roadmap)

- 7-10 Chapters (your core methodology)

- Conclusion (the transformation and call to action)

Back Matter:

- Meet the Author (position yourself as approachable expert)

- Resources (books, tools, websites you recommend)

- Thank You Note (one more connection point)

- Call to Action (leave a review, join your community)

This might seem like a lot, but each element serves a purpose. The testimonials build credibility before readers even start. The lead generation page builds your email list. The resources add value. The thank you note creates connection.

And every single element can be designed to guide readers toward your business offerings.

The Lead Generation Page: Your Book's Built-In List Builder

Let's pause here because this is critical. On one of the first few pages of your book, often right after the advance praise, you include a Lead Generation Page.

It looks something like this:

FREE BONUS: [Name of Your Bonus]

As a thank you for reading this book, I've created [describe valuable bonus] to help you [specific benefit].

This [worksheet/guide/training/template] includes:

- [Specific thing 1]

- [Specific thing 2]

- [Specific thing 3]

Get instant access at:
www.YourWebsite.com/bookbonus

This single page turns every book sale into a potential client relationship. Here's why it's brilliant:

For the reader: They get extra value, which makes them love your book even more.

For you: You capture their email address, which means you can:

- Continue the conversation after they finish the book

- Share additional value

- Invite them to your programs

- Build a relationship that leads to sales

One of our authors has sold 3,000 copies of her book. Of those, 1,200 people downloaded her bonus (40% conversion rate). From those 1,200 people, she's generated:

- 150 course sales ($297 each = $44,550)

- 25 group coaching clients ($2,000 each = $50,000)

- 8 private clients ($10,000 each = $80,000)

Total revenue from her lead magnet: $174,550

From a single page in her book.

What makes a great book bonus:

- Directly related to your book topic

- Gives a quick win or immediate value

- Demonstrates your expertise

- Naturally leads to your paid offers

- Easy to deliver (PDF, video, audio, template)

Examples:

- If your book is about productivity: "The 15-Minute Morning Routine Template"

- If your book is about marketing: "The 30-Day Content Calendar"

- If your book is about fitness: "The 7-Day Meal Plan Kickstart"

- If your book is about money: "The Budget Spreadsheet That Actually Works"

The Introduction Formula (That Sells Before Teaching)

Your introduction does three jobs: hook the reader, make a promise, and provide a roadmap. But it also does a fourth job that most authors miss: **It positions you as**

the guide they've been looking for.

Here's the exact formula:

Opening Hook (300 words): Start with a story, surprising statistic, or bold statement that makes readers lean in. This is your "you need to read this" moment.

Example opening: "Three years ago, I was $80,000 in debt, working 70-hour weeks, and heading for divorce. Today, I run a million-dollar business, work 25 hours a week, and my marriage has never been better. This book is the instruction manual I wish I'd had."

That's a hook. It promises transformation and proves you've walked the path.

The Problem (400 words): Define the problem your reader faces. Use their language, their frustrations. Make them feel understood. This is where your research from Chapter 3 pays off.

Example: "You've tried everything. The morning routines that successful people swear by. The productivity apps that promise to change your life. The time-blocking methods that look perfect on paper. And maybe they worked for a week, or even a month. But then life happened. An emergency at work. A sick kid. A project that took longer than expected. And your perfect system collapsed. Again.

You're not failing. The system is failing you. Because here's what nobody talks about: Those productivity methods were designed for a different era, a different work style, and probably a different brain than yours."

See what happened there? The reader feels understood. The problem isn't them, it's the current solutions. And you're about to offer something better.

Your Credibility (300 words): Why should they listen to you? But be careful, this isn't a resume recitation. Focus on transformation: "I went from X to Y, and here's what I learned."

Include:

- Your Point A moment (when you struggled with this same problem)

- Your breakthrough or transformation

- Results you've achieved

- Results you've helped others achieve

But keep it relevant. Your reader doesn't care that you have three degrees unless those degrees directly relate to solving their problem. They care that you've been where they are and found a way through.

The Promise (400 words): What will readers gain? Be specific. Not "you'll be happier" but "you'll have a morning routine that energizes your entire day without requiring you to wake up at 5 AM."

Break this into bullet points:

By the end of this book, you'll have:

- [Specific outcome 1]

- [Specific outcome 2]

- [Specific outcome 3]

And you'll understand:

- [Key insight 1]

- [Key insight 2]

- [Key insight 3]

More importantly, you'll be able to:

- [Practical application 1]

- [Practical application 2]

- [Practical application 3]

The Roadmap (400 words): Brief overview of each chapter or section. One to two sentences each, focusing on benefits, not topics.

Instead of: "Chapter 3 covers time management," write: "In Chapter 3, you'll discover why traditional time management fails creative people, and the rhythm-based approach that works with your brain instead of against it."

The Invitation (200 words): Close with energy and encouragement. This is where you say, "Let's do this together."

Example: "The method in this book isn't theory. It's what I've used to help over 500 clients transform their productivity without sacrificing their sanity or their soul. It's been tested in real businesses, real families, real lives. And now it's yours.

I'm excited for you. Not because this will be easy (real transformation rarely is), but because you're about to discover that the answer isn't working harder. It's working differently. Let's begin."

Total: About 2,000 words.

Enough to create momentum, not so much that readers feel overwhelmed before the real content begins.

The Chapter Blueprint (That Naturally Leads to Offers)

Every chapter follows this blueprint. Once you internalize it, chapters flow effortlessly:

Chapter Title: Clear, benefit-focused, and specific. "The 10-Minute Morning Routine That Changes Everything" beats "Morning Routines" every time.

Use formulas that work:

- "How to [Achieve Desire] Without [Common Obstacle]"

- "The [Number] [Thing] That [Impressive Result]"

- "Why [Common Approach] Fails (And What Works Instead)"

- "The [Unique Name] Method for [Solving Problem]"

Opening Quote (Optional but powerful): Choose quotes that crystallize your chapter's message, but only if they genuinely add value. Don't add quotes just to add quotes.

The Hook (300 words): Story or scenario that illustrates why this chapter matters. Start in scene: "Sarah stared at her computer screen, paralyzed by the 47 items on her to-do list. She'd been sitting there for 20 minutes, unable to decide what to tackle first. Sound familiar?"

The hook should make readers think "That's me!" or "I need to know what happens next!"

The Promise (100 words): "In this chapter, you'll discover..." Three bullet points, maximum.

Example: In this chapter, you'll discover:

- Why traditional to-do lists create paralysis instead of progress.

- The Priority Matrix that cuts decision time from 20 minutes to 2 minutes.

- How to protect your high-value work from urgent-but-not-important distractions.

Core Content Section 1 (800 words): Your first main point. Include:

- Concept explanation (what is this?)

- Why it matters (what's the impact?)

- Supporting story or case study (proof it works)

- Practical application (how to implement)

- Common mistake to avoid (what trips people up)

Business Integration Point: Within this section, include one client success story or business application. Example: "When Marcus implemented the Priority Matrix in his consulting business, he cut his work hours from 60 to 40 per week while increasing revenue by 30%. The secret wasn't doing more, it was being ruthlessly selective about what deserved his attention."

Core Content Section 2 (800 words): Your second main point, same structure.

Core Content Section 3 (800 words): Your third main point, same structure.

The Level-Up Hint: Somewhere in your core content, hint at deeper implementation. Example: "This Priority Matrix works brilliantly for most people. For business owners managing complex projects and teams, I've developed an advanced version that integrates with delegation systems and quarterly planning, my private clients use this to scale without burnout."

You're not making a sales pitch. You're simply acknowledging that there are deeper levels available for those who want them.

The Implementation Guide (500 words): Step-by-step instructions for applying what they've learned. This transforms theory into action.

Make this actionable:

Your Priority Matrix Implementation:

Step 1: Take your current to-do list and grab four colored highlighters.

Step 2: Mark each item based on the Impact/Effort Matrix:

- Green: High impact, low effort (do these first)

- Yellow: High impact, high effort (schedule these)

- Blue: Low impact, low effort (batch these)

- Pink: Low impact, high effort (eliminate or delegate these)

Step 3: Start with all green items tomorrow morning. Just the green ones.

Step 4: At the end of the day, notice how much you accomplished compared to when you worked from an undifferentiated list.

See how specific that is? Readers know exactly what to do.

Chapter Summary (300 words): 5-10 bullet points capturing key insights. Some readers skim for summaries, give them value too.

Format these as "Key Takeaways":

Key Takeaways:

- Traditional to-do lists create decision fatigue because every item appears equally important.

- The Priority Matrix uses two variables (impact and effort) to sort tasks objectively.

- High-impact, low-effort tasks should always be your starting point.

- Low-impact, high-effort tasks are the hidden time-wasters that feel productive but aren't.

- Reviewing your list with the Matrix every morning takes 2 minutes and saves hours.

Reflection Questions (200 words): 3-5 questions that deepen understanding. "How has [problem] shown up in your life?" "What would change if you implemented [solution]?"

These serve two purposes:

1. They help readers internalize the content.

2. They prime readers to want deeper support (which your coaching provides).

Example questions:

- Looking at your current to-do list, how many items would you categorize as "low impact, high effort"? What would happen if you eliminated them?

- What would you do with an extra 10 hours per week if decision fatigue wasn't consuming your energy?

- What's one high-impact project you've been postponing because it's also high-effort? What would scheduling it look like?

Your One Action (100 words): The single thing they should do after reading this chapter. Make it achievable in 15 minutes or less.

Example: "Before you sleep tonight, take 5 minutes to categorize your to-do list using the Priority Matrix. Just the categorizing, no need to reorganize anything yet. Notice what you discover about where your time is really going."

Total per chapter: About 3,500 words.

Substantial enough to deliver value, short enough to maintain attention.

Real Author Insights: What Works in Structure

From our author interviews, here's what people said

about structure:

On chapter length: "I worried my chapters were too short. Then readers told me they loved that they could finish a chapter in one sitting. Short chapters created momentum." – Business coach

"I made my first draft chapters way too long, 8,000 words each. When I broke them into 3,000-word chapters, the whole book felt more accessible." – Marketing consultant

On structure: "The action steps at the end of each chapter were the most valuable part according to my readers. They loved having clear next steps." – Productivity expert

"I didn't include reflection questions in my first draft. My editor insisted. Those questions generated the most social media engagement when readers shared their answers." – Life coach

On the business connection: "I was subtle about my services in the book, maybe too subtle. Readers finished the book wanting more but didn't know how to work with me. In the second edition, I added a clear path." – Consultant

"My biggest surprise was how many readers went from book to high-ticket offer without buying anything in between. I thought I needed a step-by-step ascension. Turns out, the right readers knew they wanted the premium option immediately." – Executive coach

Learn from their experiences. Structure matters. Clarity matters. And making it easy for readers to continue the journey with you? That really matters.

The Conclusion That Converts (Readers to Clients)

Your conclusion isn't an ending, it's a beginning. It transforms readers from consumers of your content to implementers of your method, and potentially clients of your services.

The Journey Review (400 words): Remind them where they started and how far they've come just by reading.

Example: "When you opened this book, you were [description of their Point A]. You felt [emotion]. You struggled with [problem]. You'd tried [failed solutions].

Now, you understand [key insight 1]. You have [tool 1] and [tool 2]. You know [new perspective]. You're no longer [old limiting belief]. You're someone who [new identity]."

This isn't fluff. This is acknowledgment of their journey. And it reinforces the transformation your book provides, which is a preview of the even greater transformation your services provide.

The Transformation Vision (400 words): Paint a picture

of their life when they implement what they've learned. Make it vivid and specific.

Example: "Imagine waking up tomorrow and knowing exactly what deserves your attention. No more decision fatigue. No more three-hour marathon work sessions that leave you drained. Instead, you work in focused 90-minute blocks, accomplish more by noon than you used to in a full day, and have energy left for the people and projects that matter.

Your team knows what's important because you're no longer treating every task as equally urgent. Your clients notice the difference, you're more present, more strategic, more effective. Your family gets the best of you, not the exhausted leftovers. This isn't fantasy. It's what happens when you consistently apply the Priority Matrix and the other tools in this book."

Make the vision compelling. Make it real. Make them want it.

The Success Path (400 words): Next steps, in order. What should they do first, second, third?

Example: "Here's your path forward:

This Week: Implement the Priority Matrix every morning. Just this one tool will create noticeable change.

This Month: Add the Energy Mapping technique from Chapter 5. Start scheduling high-impact work during your peak energy windows.

Next Three Months: Build out your complete Productivity Operating System using all seven tools from this book. Track your results. Refine what works for you.

Ongoing: Join our community of readers implementing these methods. Share your wins, ask questions, and support others on the same journey."

The Community Invitation (300 words): How to stay connected, get support, and continue learning. This is where you mention your courses, coaching, or community, but from a service perspective, not a sales perspective.

Example: "You don't have to do this alone. In fact, you'll get better results with support.

Free Resources:

- Join our Facebook community: [link]

- Weekly implementation tips: [newsletter signup]

- My podcast for deeper dives: [link]

Accelerated Implementation:

- Online Course: If you want guided implementation with video training, templates, and group coaching, check out [Course Name] at [link]. It's the next step for people who want structured support.

- Private Coaching: If you're ready for personalized strategy and accountability, I work with a small number of private clients. Learn more at [link].

- Group Mastermind: Four times a year, I host a small group of high-performers who want to optimize their productivity while building meaningful businesses. If you're interested, join the waitlist at [link].

Choose the path that feels right for your stage and goals. Any path you choose, I'm honored to be part of your journey."

See how that works? You're not pushing. You're offering options. You're meeting people where they are.

The Final Rally (200 words): Your parting words of encouragement. Make them feel capable and excited.

Example: "I believe in you. I believe in your goals, your dreams, your ability to create something extraordinary. Not because you're working harder, but because you're about to work differently.

Everything you need is in these pages. The rest is up to you. But here's what I know: If you implement even half of what you've learned, your life will change. And if you implement everything? You'll be unstoppable.

The world needs what you're building. Don't let productivity challenges stand in your way.

Now go. Build. Create. Transform.

I can't wait to hear your success story.

[Your Name]"

Total conclusion: About 1,700 words.

Short enough to maintain energy, but long enough to inspire action and provide clear next steps.

The Secret Weapon: Modular Writing (That Multiplies Your Content)

Here's what makes this system magical: You don't have to write in order.

Each element, each story, each how-to section, each reflection question, is a module. You can write them in any order and assemble them later. Feeling inspired about Chapter 6? Write it. Have a great story for Chapter 2? Capture it.

One of our authors wrote her entire book in what she called "snippet sessions," 15-minute writing bursts focused on one module. She'd write one story, one how-to section, one summary. Over six weeks of snippet sessions, she had a complete book.

This approach eliminates writer's block because you're never facing "write Chapter 3." You're facing "Write the story about the time you learned about resilience" or "Explain the three types of morning routines." Small, specific, achievable.

But here's the multiplier effect: Each snippet can

be repurposed.

That story you wrote for Chapter 3? It becomes:

- Part of your book

- A social media post while you're writing

- An email to your list

- Part of your lead magnet

- An example in your course

- A podcast episode story

- Content for a blog post

One writing session. Seven uses. That's efficiency.

The Content Multiplication Strategy (From One Book to Entire Business Ecosystem)

Every piece of content can serve multiple purposes. That story about overcoming fear? It could be:

- **A chapter opener** (you've already done this)

- **A social media post** while you're writing (building anticipation)

- **A newsletter** to your audience (engaging your community)

- **Part of your book proposal** (if you're seeking

traditional publishing)

- **An example in your course** (visual content showing the concept)

- **A podcast episode** (expanding on the story with more detail)

- **A keynote speech opener** (you get paid to tell your story)

- **Your "signature story"** (the one you're known for)

This isn't just efficiency—it's strategic brand building. When people hear the same story across multiple platforms, it becomes associated with you. It becomes your "thing." And your "thing" becomes your brand.

Simar shared our "Clear Not Clever" title concept in a workshop before the book was done. The response was so strong, we knew it would be a key selling point. Your audience tells you what they want. Listen, then multiply it across channels.

Your Business Blueprint Disguised as a Book Outline

Here's what we want you to see: **Your book outline IS your business blueprint.**

Let me show you:

Book Chapter 1: The problem you solve and why current

solutions fail.

Business Application: This becomes your marketing message and the foundation of your sales conversations.

Book Chapter 2: Your unique framework or methodology.

Business Application: This becomes your signature system that you teach in courses and coaching.

Book Chapter 3: Step one of implementation.

Business Application: This becomes Module 1 of your course and session 1 of your group program.

Book Chapters 4-7: Steps two through five of implementation.

Business Application: Modules 2-5 of your course, the framework for your workshops.

Book Chapter 8: Advanced strategies and avoiding pitfalls.

Business Application: Bonus module in your course, topics for private coaching sessions.

Book Conclusion: Next level transformation.

Business Application: The promise of your high-ticket coaching or done-for-you services.

One outline. Two purposes. Maximum efficiency.

This is why we say: Write the Book, Build the Business, Be the Brand. They're not separate activities. They're the same activity from different angles.

Download our Book Outline Template at
LuckyBookPublishing.com/book

Your Assignment: Create Your Complete Outline

Before moving to the next chapter, complete your full book outline using our template.

Front Matter:

- Lead magnet title and description

- 3-5 advance praise testimonials you'll seek

Introduction:

- Hook: Your opening story or statement

- The problem in one paragraph

- Your credibility in one paragraph

- Your promise: 3 specific outcomes

- Chapter overview: One sentence per chapter

Chapter Outlines (for each of 7-10 chapters):

- Chapter title

- Opening hook story (one sentence description)

- Main Point 1 + example

- Main Point 2 + example

- Main Point 3 + example

- One Action step

- Business integration point

Conclusion:

- Journey review theme

- Vision of transformation

- Next steps (1, 2, 3)

- Offer mentions

This outline becomes your roadmap. With this level of detail, writing becomes assembly. You're not creating from nothing, you're filling in a framework that's already solid.

And that framework? It's not just your book. It's your business model in outline form.

Tag us @LuckyBookPublishing
when your author journey begins.
We would love to celebrate with you!

Guiding Speakers to their Golden Ticket

TERI KINGSTON

TEDxCoach, Author

When Teri Kingston set out to write *Get Ready for TED When TED is Ready for YOU!*, she wanted to create a travel companion for those dreaming of a TEDx stage, a book that would simplify a complex process and empower speakers to share their "idea worth spreading." What she didn't expect was how much it would transform her own coaching practice.

Partnering with Lucky Book Publishing helped Teri cut through the noise of multiple ideas and focus on the one she was most qualified to teach, the questions her clients asked every day. That clarity became her Table of Contents, and the book soon became both a guide and a credential.

Today, *Get Ready for TED* has positioned Teri as a trusted authority in the TEDx coaching world, attracting clients worldwide and opening doors to podcasts, webinars, and conferences. Her message is simple yet catalytic: *Your story deserves a stage*.

Connect with Teri Kingston:
🌐 RealImpactSpeaking.com
✉ info@realimpactspeaking.com

Your Life Matters

HAL EISENBERG

Educator, Author, Keynote Speaker

When I self-published my first book, *Beautiful Soul*, I had no idea what I was doing. I poured my heart into it but made every mistake possible, rushing the process, overlooking details, and trying to do it all alone. It was raw and real, but I knew there had to be a better way to bring my message to life.

But *Whispers in the Rain* came from my healing. I had been praying for a sign, asking the universe if I should release these 48 sacred spiritual lessons. Then I met Simar at a conference in Toronto, and everything shifted. The universe answered by placing the exact right person in front of me at the exact right time.

Working with Lucky Book Publishing was a completely different experience. From the very first conversation, I felt supported, guided, and understood. They didn't just help me publish a book; they helped me uncover the soul of my message. Together, we transformed my lessons into something bigger, creating a global movement of healing.

The most powerful moment was when Simar said, "This book is going to change lives." Not *sell well, change lives*. That was the turning point. Lucky Book Publishing gave me permission to step fully into my purpose and reminded me that every story has a soul and that *your life truly matters*.

Connect with Hal Eisenberg:
🌐 Haleisenberg.com
📷 hal_eisenberg88

5

The Clear Not Clever Title Formula

Your title is not the place to be creative.

We know that's hard to hear. You want something memorable, something that shows your personality. But here's what we've learned from hundreds of book launches: clear titles sell, clever titles sit on shelves.

Your title has one job: Tell potential readers what problem your book solves in language they use when searching for solutions. That's it.

The 5-Second Test

A potential reader sees your book on Amazon, on a social media post, on a shelf. They give it five seconds of attention, maximum. In those five seconds, they need to understand:

1. What this book is about.

2. Whether it's for them.

3. What benefit they'll get from reading it.

If they have to think about your title, decode it, or wonder what it means, you've lost them.

Atomic Habits passes the test. You know it's about habits, and "atomic" suggests small but powerful.

How to Win Friends and Influence People passes brilliantly. The entire benefit is in the title.

The Life-Changing Magic of Tidying Up tells you exactly what you'll get.

These aren't creative titles. They're clear titles. And they've sold millions of copies.

The Title Formula That Works

After analyzing bestsellers across every non-fiction category, we've identified the formula:

[Benefit] + [Specific Method/Approach] + [Target Audience Identifier]

Not every title needs all three elements, but the best ones have at least two.

Examples:

- *The 4-Hour Workweek* = Benefit (work less) + Specific Method (4 hours)

- *Rich Dad Poor Dad* = Specific Method (contrasting approaches) + Benefit (implied wealth)

- *You Are a Badass at Making Money* = Target Audience (you) + Benefit (making money)

The Subtitle Power Play

Your subtitle does the heavy lifting. While your title hooks attention, your subtitle closes the sale. It expands on the promise and specifies who should read this book.

Subtitle formula:

[Specific Process/Method] + [To Achieve Specific Result] + [For Specific Audience]

Real examples:

- *Atomic Habits: An Easy & Proven Way to Build Good Habits & Break Bad Ones*

- *The Subtle Art of Not Giving a F*ck: A Counterintuitive Approach to Living a Good Life*

- *Girl, Wash Your Face: Stop Believing the Lies About Who You Are So You Can Become Who You Were Meant to Be*

Notice how specific these are. They don't leave readers wondering.

The Keyword Research Process

Before finalizing your title, you need to know what words your readers actually use. This isn't guessing, it's research.

Step 1: Amazon Categories

Go to Amazon. Navigate to your book's category. Look at the bestsellers. What words appear repeatedly in titles? These are proven keywords.

Step 2: Google Autocomplete

Type "how to [your topic]" into Google. See what autocompletes. These are actual searches people make. Do the same with "why does," "what is," "when should I."

Step 3: AnswerThePublic

This free tool shows you every question people ask about your topic. The exact language they use becomes your title and chapter headings.

Step 4: Facebook Groups and Forums

Join groups where your ideal readers hang out. What phrases do they use repeatedly? What questions come up over and over? One author found her perfect title "Midnight Mom Devotions" from a phrase used repeatedly in a moms' group.

Step 5: Review Mining

Read reviews of competing books. What language do satisfied readers use? What do disappointed readers say was missing? Your title can position your book as the answer.

Ready to name your book?
Try our Clear-Not-Clever Title Formula Worksheet
LuckyBookPublishing.com/book

The Testing Protocol

Never commit to a title without testing. Here's our proven testing process:

The Social Media Test:

Post three potential titles in relevant groups with this script: "I'm finalizing my book title and would love your input. Which of these would you be most likely to buy?"

- Option A: [Title + Subtitle]

- Option B: [Title + Subtitle]

- Option C: [Title + Subtitle]

The responses tell you everything. Not just the votes, but

the comments. Someone might say, "I'd buy A, but only if it covers X." That's gold.

The Stranger Test:

Tell someone you just met you're writing a book. Say the title. If they immediately get it and show interest, you're on track. If they look confused or you have to explain, keep refining.

The Search Test:

Search your potential title on Amazon. If 50 books come up with the exact same title, you need to differentiate. If zero books come up, make sure you're not using language nobody searches for.

Common Title Mistakes to Avoid

Mistake 1: Being Too Clever

Eat, Pray, Love worked for Elizabeth Gilbert because she was already established. For your first book, skip the poetry. Be clear.

Mistake 2: Being Too Broad

How to Be Happy is too general. *How to Find Joy After Divorce* speaks to a specific person with a specific need.

Mistake 3: Using Jargon

Unless your audience uses technical terms daily, avoid them in your title. *Optimizing Your Metabolic Performance* loses to *Boost Your Metabolism in 30 Days*.

Mistake 4: Making It About You

My Journey to Success makes it about you. *Your Journey to Success* makes it about them. Guess which sells better?

Mistake 5: Forgetting SEO

Your title needs to work in digital searches. Include words people actually type into search bars.

The Evolution Process

Your title will evolve, and that's okay. Start with a working title that captures the essence. As you write, you'll discover the real hook of your book.

One author started with *Leadership Lessons from Corporate Life*. Through writing, she discovered her unique angle was about leading without authority. Her final title: *The Influence Effect: How to Lead When You're Not in Charge*. Much more specific, much more powerful.

Keep a title journal as you write. When you have an idea, write it down. When you hear a phrase that resonates, capture it. Your perfect title often emerges during the writing process, not before it.

Your story deserves to be shared.
Let's publish it together.
Book your author strategy call today.
LuckyBookPublishing.com/work-with-us

From Page to Stage
Narcolepsy is My Strength

Michelle Weger

Productivity & Resilience Expert

When Michelle Weger sat down to write Don't Snooze Your Dreams, she wasn't just writing a book, she was building a bridge. "I wanted to help dreamers become doers," she said. "Because potential means nothing if you keep hitting snooze on your own life."

As the founder of a thriving business, Michelle knew what it meant to juggle ambition and overwhelm. But it wasn't until she began working with Lucky Book Publishing that her scattered ideas became a clear, empowering roadmap. "Sam and Simar helped me see that I didn't have to be perfect, I just had to be present," she shared. "They reminded me that my story already had power."

Through the process, Michelle learned that clarity breeds confidence. "I wrote the book I wish I had when I was starting out," she said. "It's for every person who's ever had a dream that felt too big, too far, or too late."

From page to stage around the world, Don't Snooze Your Dreams is igniting conversations about courage, resilience and productivity. Michelle continues to coach and mentor leaders who are ready to take bold, aligned action. "Wake up," she reminds all of us. "Your dreams are waiting for you."

Connect with Michelle Weger:

🌐 michelleweger.com
📷 @michelleaweger

Finding the Courage to Be Fully Seen

JENN NOBLE

PCC, Relationship Coach, TEDx Speaker, Podcast Host, Bestselling Author of Dance of Attachment

When Jenn Noble wrote *Dance of Attachment: Why Smart Women Do Dumb Sh*t in Relationships and How to Break the Pattern*, she thought she was writing for others, but in truth, she was giving herself permission to feel, heal, and be seen. The process cracked her open, shifting her from performer to truth-teller, and her #1 bestselling book became a mirror for women everywhere learning to do the same.

Partnering with Lucky Book Publishing helped Jenn find the clarity and courage to lead with her passion. As Sam told her, *"The world needs to hear your passion,"* and once Jenn stopped trying to sound polished and started sounding real, everything changed. The message got bigger, the brand got bolder, and she finally felt like herself.

Today, *Dance of Attachment* is more than a book, it's a movement, giving women language for what they've always felt and permission to take up space in love, life, and leadership.

Connect with Jennifer Noble:
🌐 SpeakHonest.com
✉ info@speakhonest.com

Using Words as a Bridge Between Healing and Belonging

NAVREET PABLA

Author and Poet

When Navreet Pabla began writing *If My Heart Could Talk*, she thought her poems were meant to stay private, until she realized the power of releasing them. Publishing the book felt like unlocking a drawer in her heart. As her words found their way into the world, readers found themselves reflected in them. Her vulnerability became a bridge, reminding her and others—that no one heals alone.

Partnering with Lucky Book Publishing helped Navreet silence the voice of doubt and share her story with confidence. *"Don't be a best-kept secret,"* they told her, and that reminder changed everything. Writing became an act of courage; publishing became an act of service.

Today, Navreet's poetry is inspiring readers and sparking honest conversations around healing, identity, and self-expression. Her words invite others to soften, to speak, and to come home to themselves. *If my heart could talk, it would tell you: yours was never broken—just asking to be heard.*

Connect with Navreet Pabla:
navreet.pabla
hello@navreetpabla.com

6

The Cover That Sells

Your cover is not art. It's advertising.

This might be the hardest mindset shift for authors. You want something beautiful, something that represents your book's essence. But a cover that sells has one job: Stop the scroll and communicate value in under three seconds.

The Three-Part Test

Every successful book cover passes three tests:

Test 1: It grabs attention

In a sea of books, whether physical or digital, yours needs to stand out. This doesn't mean garish or loud. It means visually distinctive.

Test 2: The title and subtitle are readable

As a thumbnail on Amazon. On someone's phone screen. From across a bookstore. If people can't read your title, they won't buy your book.

Test 3: Your ideal reader instantly understands what it's about

The design, colors, fonts, and imagery should telegraph genre and topic immediately. A business book shouldn't look like a romance novel. A parenting book shouldn't look like a thriller.

The Nine Cover Archetypes

Through analyzing thousands of successful non-fiction covers, we've identified nine archetypes that consistently perform:

1. Classic Design

Clean, professional, often with geometric elements. Perfect for business, finance, and leadership books. Think *Good to Great* or *The Lean Startup*.

2. Intellectual

Sophisticated typography, muted colors, plenty of white space. Signals depth and research. Malcolm Gladwell's books exemplify this style.

3. Thought Leader

Often features the author's photo. Works when you have an established platform or powerful personal brand. Brené Brown and Tony Robbins use this approach.

4. Illustration

Custom illustrations or icons that represent your concept. Great for making complex ideas approachable. *Atomic Habits* uses this brilliantly with its simple atomic symbol.

5. Type-Driven

The typography IS the design. Bold, impossible to ignore. *The Subtle Art of Not Giving a F*ck* made this approach famous.

6. Minimal

Maximum white space, minimal elements. Signals confidence and clarity. Often used for mindfulness, meditation, and simplicity topics.

7. Hand-Drawn Type

Adds personality and approachability. Perfect for creative topics, personal development, and books targeting younger audiences.

8. Maverick

Breaks category conventions intentionally. Risky but can be powerful if your book's positioning is truly different.

9. Photo-Based

A powerful photograph that captures your book's essence. Works for memoirs, travel, and transformation stories.

The Design Brief That Gets Results

Before creating your cover, complete this design brief. It becomes your north star for all design decisions:

1. Author Name(s)

How do you want your name displayed? Full name? Initials? Include credentials?

2. Book Title

Exact wording, including capitalization preferences.

3. Book Subtitle

Every word matters. Triple-check for typos.

4. Additional Cover Text

Endorsement quotes? "Bestselling Author of..." lines? Edition information?

5. Primary Emotion

What should readers feel when they see your cover? Inspired? Curious? Confident? Comforted? Choose one primary emotion.

6. Visual Ideas

Describe any imagery that captures your book's essence. Be specific but not prescriptive.

7. Colour Psychology

- Red: Energy, urgency, passion

- Blue: Trust, stability, wisdom

- Green: Growth, health, prosperity

- Yellow: Optimism, creativity, warmth

- Purple: Luxury, spirituality, creativity

- Orange: Enthusiasm, adventure, confidence

- Black: Sophistication, authority, elegance

- White: Simplicity, purity, possibility

8. Competitor Analysis

Find 3-5 successful books in your category. What do their covers have in common? How can yours fit the category while standing out?

9. The Bookshelf Test

Imagine your book on a shelf next to competitors. Does it blend in or stand out? You want to fit the category enough that readers recognize what it is, but be distinctive enough to catch attention.

The Typography Rules

Typography can make or break your cover. Here are non-negotiable rules:

Rule 1: Contrast Is King

Light text on dark background or dark text on light background. Never medium on medium.

Rule 2: Hierarchy Matters

Title should be the largest element. Subtitle smaller but still readable. Author name can be smaller unless you're well-known.

Rule 3: Limit Font Families

Two maximum. Usually one for the title, one for everything else. More than two looks amateur.

Rule 4: Test at Thumbnail Size

Your cover will most often be seen as a tiny image on a screen. If the title isn't readable at thumbnail size, start over.

Rule 5: Avoid Thin Fonts

They disappear at small sizes and don't photograph well for social media posts.

The Colour Strategy

Colour isn't only about what you like, it's about what works:

Stand Out in Your Category

If every book in your category is blue and white, consider orange or green. You want to fit the genre but catch the eye.

Consider Colour Psychology

Your colour choices send subconscious messages. A book about financial success probably shouldn't be purple (unless you're deliberately breaking convention).

Test in Different Contexts

Your cover needs to work:

- As a thumbnail on Amazon

- In black and white (some e-readers)

- On social media feeds

- In email signatures

- On business cards

Have questions about your book cover?
DM us on Instagram @LuckyBookPublishing,
we'd love to help you out!

The Amateur Mistakes to Avoid

Mistake 1: DIY When You Shouldn't

Unless you're a professional designer, hire one. A homemade cover screams "amateur" and suggests the content might be too.

Mistake 2: Too Many Elements

Every element should earn its place. If it doesn't add value, remove it.

Mistake 3: Trendy Fonts

That cool font everyone's using today will look dated next year. Stick with proven, timeless typography.

Mistake 4: Literal Interpretation

Your book about time management doesn't need a clock on the cover. Think deeper about visual metaphors.

Mistake 5: Ignoring the Spine

If you're printing physical books, the spine needs your title and author name, readable from a distance.

The Testing Protocol

Never go to print without testing your cover:

The Five-Foot Test

Print your cover and prop it five feet away. Can you read the title? Does it draw your eye?

The Thumbnail Test

Shrink your cover to thumbnail size. Is everything still clear? Does it still have impact?

The Social Media Test

Post your cover (or top 3 options) in relevant groups. Ask: "Based on the cover alone, what do you think this book is about?" If they guess wrong, revise.

The Category Test

Screenshot your book cover among bestsellers in your category. Does it fit while standing out?

Tag us @LuckyBookPublishing when
you start your author journey!
We love lifting you higher!

Rediscovering Purpose

CHARLES ACHAMPONG

Executive in Residence, Author and Speaker

For Charles Achampong, writing *Around the World in Family Days* wasn't about documenting travel—it was about rediscovering presence. What began as a personal story of family adventures evolved into a lesson in clarity, resilience, and intentional living. The real transformation wasn't about geography; it was about giving himself permission to slow down and listen.

Partnering with Lucky Book Publishing helped Charles refine his story so that its deeper message—*the courage to pause*—took center stage. *"You don't have to earn your worth by running yourself into the ground,"* he says. That realization changed everything.

Today, his book and message are opening doors to global conversations about leadership, balance, and redefining success. For Charles, the power of pausing is no longer just a theme—it's a way of leading, living, and inspiring others to do the same.

Connect with Charles Achampong:
🌐 CharlesAchampong.com
📷 aroundtheworldinfamilydays

Making the Uncomfortable, Comfortable

HEATHER COLEMAN

*MBA, PMP, Financial Wellness Geek &
#1 Bestselling Author*

For Heather Coleman, writing *Our Money Narrative & The Impacts on Our Financial Wellness* was turning on the high beams during a foggy drive. A TEDx speaker and financial wellness expert, she'd spent years helping others manage their money—but this time, the journey was inward. Writing forced her to confront her own beliefs about money, worth, and what financial freedom really means.

Partnering with Lucky Book Publishing helped Heather find her voice and her vision. She discovered that you can stay true to your authentic self *and* tell a story that matters. Publishing didn't just build her brand—it built a movement. Readers began saying, "You made the uncomfortable, comfortable," and Heather knew her words were doing their work.

Today, her mission is clear: to help people rewrite their money stories with courage, clarity, and compassion—because our financial wellness begins with the narratives we tell ourselves.

Connect with Heather Coleman:
🌐 HeatherColeman.ca
✉ heather@heathercoleman.ca

Turning Lessons into Legacy

MELISSA GUENETTE MASON

*CEO, A-List Media Solutions, Marketing and PR
Specialist, Bestselling Author*

For over two decades, Melissa Guenette Mason built brands behind the scenes— building strategies, shaping voices, and helping others shine. But writing *Start From Experience* changed everything. Holding her own book for the first time wasn't just a professional milestone—it was personal proof of her voice, her vision, and her journey.

Partnering with Lucky Book Publishing gave Melissa the structure and encouragement to step into her own spotlight. She learned that vulnerability connects just as powerfully as strategy, and that a book isn't just a product— it's a platform. The result? A #1 bestseller that opened doors to speaking engagements, media features, and collaborations, transforming how the world sees her and how she sees herself.

Her message is clear and timeless: *Every mistake carries wisdom, and every setback shapes what's next*. You don't need a perfect plan—you just need the courage to keep moving.

Connect with Melissa Guenette Mason:
🌐 AListMediaSolutions.com
✉ media@alistmediasolutions.com

Part Three: The Launch

7

Building Your Book Squad

Before you write a single word of your book, you need to start building what we call your Book Squad—the 200 people who will make your launch successful.

This isn't about having a massive social media following. It's about creating genuine connections with people who care about your topic and want to see you succeed.

The 200-Person Strategy

Why 200? It's the sweet spot. Enough to create momentum, not so many that you can't maintain real relationships.

These aren't just email addresses. These are people you've personally connected with who are genuinely interested in your book. They'll be your:

- Beta readers

- Early reviewers

- Launch day buyers

- Word-of-mouth spreaders

- Ongoing champions

Here's the truth most people won't tell you: An engaged squad of 200 beats a passive email list of 10,000 every time.

Samantha learned this early in her career, long before Lucky Book Publishing existed. While leading leadership circles and networking events, she noticed something powerful. It wasn't the biggest rooms that created the biggest breakthroughs, it was the most connected ones. When people came together to share experiences, lift each other up, and collaborate instead of compete, entire careers shifted. Those experiences taught her that real impact comes from authentic connections, not just large numbers.

The Connection Calendar

Starting today, commit to making five new connections per week. Not mass connections—real ones.

Monday: Facebook Groups

Join one new group related to your topic. Don't promote. Just show up, answer questions, add value. People will naturally ask about you.

Tuesday: Comment Deeply

Find five posts in your groups or on LinkedIn. Leave thoughtful comments that add to the conversation. Not "Great post!" but real engagement.

Wednesday: Direct Outreach

Send five personal messages to people you'd like to connect with. Tell them what you appreciated about their content. Ask a thoughtful question. Start a conversation.

Thursday: Content Sharing

Share one piece of valuable content—yours or someone else's—with a personal note about why it matters. Tag people who would benefit.

Friday: Gratitude Practice

Thank five people publicly. Maybe they inspired your book idea. Maybe they answered a question. Public gratitude creates powerful connections.

Five connections per week equals 20 per month. In 10 months, you have your 200.

The Behind-the-Curtain Strategy

People don't just want to read your book—they want to be part of your journey. Share the process.

This insight came from watching traditional publishers completely miss the mark. They'd keep books secret until launch day, then wonder why no one cared. We watched indie musicians build massive followings by sharing studio sessions, works in progress, the messy middle of creation. Why couldn't authors do the same?

Our first experiment with this was author number eighteen, a former chef writing about career transformation. She was terrified. "What if people steal my ideas?" she worried. "What if they judge my rough drafts?"

We convinced her to try it for one month. Just share the journey, we said. See what happens.

Her first post was simple: A photo of her laptop and coffee cup with the caption, "Chapter 1, Day 1. Writing about the day I walked out of a Michelin-starred kitchen and into unemployment. Scared then, scared now, but for different reasons."

Seventeen comments within an hour. Not judgment—support. Not theft but engagement. People sharing their own career change stories, cheering her on, asking to be notified when the book was ready.

By the time she finished writing three months later, she had 500 people waiting to buy her book. They'd watched her struggle through Chapter 4, celebrated when she figured out her title, offered suggestions when she got stuck on her conclusion.

They weren't just readers—they were invested participants in her journey.

Week 1: Announce Your Intention

"I'm writing a book about [topic]. It's for [ideal reader] who struggles with [problem]. Would love your input as I write!"

The announcement itself is powerful. It makes it real. Samantha remembers posting her first book announcement with shaking hands. Once it was out there, there was no taking it back. The accountability was immediate and powerful.

Week 2: Share Your Research

"Fascinating statistic I discovered while researching my book..." or "Just interviewed an expert who said something that changed my perspective..."

This works because you're providing value while building anticipation. You're not just talking about writing a book—you're sharing useful information that happens to come from your book research. One author shared a statistic about workplace stress that got reshared 200 times. Those 200 shares became 200 potential readers who knew she was writing a book on the topic.

Week 3: Vulnerable Moment

"Struggling with Chapter 3 today. How do you explain [concept] without being preachy?" People love helping.

We discovered this accidentally when Simar posted in frustration about trying to explain the difference between clear and clever titles. She wasn't looking for help —just venting. But the responses were gold. Real readers telling her exactly what confused them about book titles, what they looked for, what made them buy or pass. That Facebook vent session became the foundation for our entire title chapter.

Week 4: Celebration

"Just finished Chapter 5! Here's a snippet that I'm particularly proud of..." Share a paragraph, not a chapter.

Celebrations invite people to share your joy. They create emotional investment. When you finally launch, these people feel like they were part of creating something, not just consuming it.

This weekly rhythm keeps people engaged without overwhelming them. They feel part of the process, not marketed to.

We've watched authors try to hide their process, thinking mystery creates anticipation. It doesn't. It creates indifference. People support what they help create. They champion what they feel part of. They buy from people they've watched struggle and succeed.

Need help turning your book into a business?
Join our next *Write the Book
That Changes Everything* workshop at
LuckyBookPublishing.com/events

The Lead Generation Machine

You need a way to capture interested people's contact information. This is your lead generation page—a simple one-page website that offers something valuable in exchange for an email address.

The Formula:

Headline: The benefit they'll get

Subheadline: Who it's for and what problem it solves

Bullet Points: 3-5 specific things they'll learn

Opt-in Form: Name and email only

Call to Action: Clear, benefit-focused button text

Example:

Headline: "The 5-Minute Morning Routine That Transforms Your Entire Day"

Subheadline: "For overwhelmed professionals who want to start their day with energy and focus instead of chaos and coffee."

Bullets:

- The 3-step wake-up sequence that eliminates grogginess

- How to protect your morning from email and social media

- The one question that clarifies your entire day's priorities

Button: "Send Me The Morning Routine!"

What do you offer? It could be:

- A chapter from your book

- A checklist or worksheet

- A video training

- An audio recording

- A resource list

The key: It should be valuable enough to stand alone but leave them wanting more—more that your book will provide.

The Beta Reader System

Beta readers are gold. They're early readers who give you feedback before you publish. But more importantly, they become emotionally invested in your book's success.

Here's how to build your beta reader team:

Six Months Before Launch:

Post in your groups: "I'm looking for 20 beta readers for my upcoming book about [topic]. You'll get the book free, early, and your feedback will shape the final version. Interested?"

Selection Process:

Don't take everyone. Ask interested people:

1. What interests you about this topic?

2. What would you hope to learn from this book?

3. Can you commit to reading it within two weeks and providing feedback?

Choose people who give thoughtful responses and represent your ideal reader.

The Beta Package:

Send them:

- The manuscript (watermarked PDF)

- Specific questions to answer

- A deadline for feedback

- A thank you and promise to acknowledge them in the book

Beta Questions That Get Useful Feedback:

1. What was your biggest takeaway from the book?

2. Was anything confusing or unclear?

3. What did you want more of?

4. What could be cut without losing value?

5. Would you recommend this to a friend? Why or why not?

6. What would you title this book?

7. Who specifically should read this?

The Beta Reader Payoff:

Your beta readers become your launch team. They've invested time in your book. They want to see it succeed. They'll be your first reviewers, your most enthusiastic promoters.

The Advance Praise Strategy

Those quotes you see on book covers and in the front matter? They don't appear magically. They're strategically gathered months before launch.

Step 1: Create Your Hit List

List 20-30 people whose endorsement would matter to your readers. Include:

- Authors in your genre

- Experts in your field

- People with platforms your audience respects

- Previous clients or students (if applicable)

- Thought leaders in adjacent fields

Step 2: The Approach Email

Subject: Quick Question About [Their Recent Work/Achievement]

Hi [Name],

I just finished [their recent book/article/interview] and was particularly struck by your insight about [specific detail]. It perfectly relates to something I've been exploring in my upcoming book.

I'm writing [Book Title], which helps [target audience] achieve [benefit]. Your work on [their expertise] has significantly influenced my thinking, particularly [specific example].

Would you be open to reading an advance copy? If it resonates, I'd be honored to include your endorsement, but there's absolutely no obligation.

Either way, thank you for the work you do. It matters.

Best,

[Your name]

Step 3: The Follow-Up Package

If they say yes, send:

- A PDF of your book (or relevant chapters)

- A one-page summary of key points

- A soft deadline (3-4 weeks)

- Sample endorsements for inspiration (not to copy)

Step 4: Make It Easy

When they agree to endorse, offer to draft something for their approval. Many busy people appreciate this. "Would it be helpful if I drafted something based on your feedback? You can edit it however you like or write your own."

The Pre-Launch Momentum

Three months before launch, shift into active pre-launch mode:

Month 3: Announce Your Launch Date

Create anticipation. "Mark your calendars! [Book Title] launches [Date]. Here's what you can expect..."

Month 2: Share Snippets

Weekly posts with valuable excerpts. Each should stand alone as useful content while creating desire for more.

Month 1: Build the Countdown

Daily value posts related to your book's topic. Share stories, tips, behind-the-scenes moments. Create momentum that builds to launch day.

Proving That Growth Has No Expiration Date

SHELLEY A. MURDOCK

Author and Longevity Coach

For Shelley A. Murdock, writing *In Search of Longevity* and *Healthy & Fit for Life* wasn't just about sharing wellness strategies. It was about proving that growth has no expiration date. Becoming an author at 65 transformed her life, her business, and her sense of purpose. What began as a personal mission to live well evolved into a platform for helping others engineer healthy, joyful, and sustainable lives.

Partnering with Lucky Book Publishing helped Shelley clarify her message and step into visibility. *"Get out of your own way,"* Sam and Simar told her, and that simple truth changed everything. She realized that selling her book wasn't about self-promotion—it was about service.

Today, Shelley leads workshops, speaks at conferences, and inspires audiences worldwide to move, breathe, and live with vitality. Her legacy is clear: wellness isn't about quick fixes or age limits—it's about purpose in motion and health that lasts a lifetime.

Connect with Shelley A. Murdock:
🌐 FitnessWithShell.com
✉ info@fitnesswithshell.com

From Dreaming to Done

NADIA S. KRAUSS

Soul Health Mentor & Co

When Nadia S. Krauss began writing *From Dreaming to Done: A Soul Map for Finishing What You Were Born to Do*, she was being called to evolve — from seeker to creator, from student to founder. The book became more than a manuscript; it became the vessel for her Soul Map Spiral™ methodology, a framework for helping others complete what their soul began.

Partnering with Lucky Book Publishing helped Nadia see her book not as separate from her business, but as her *Authority Primer*. Through their From Idea to Book Framework and collaborative feedback, she found the clarity to claim her unique "Category of One."

Even before publication, *From Dreaming to Done* is opening doors—to keynotes, collaborations, and podcast invitations. Readers already call it "nourishment" and "permission to finish." Nadia's message is clear and catalytic: *Don't die with a dream still living inside you.*

Connect with Nadia S. Krauss:
🌐 SoulHealthMentor.com
✉ info@soulhealthmentor.com

8
The Ripple Effect Strategy

Your book launch isn't a day—it's a system designed to create ripples that expand outward for months and years.

Most authors think launch day is the finish line. Actually, it's the starting gun. Everything you've done up to this point has been preparing for the ripple effect: Your book reaching readers who reach other readers who reach other readers.

The Launch Squad Activation

Remember those 200 people in your Book Squad? Launch week is their moment to shine.

Two Weeks Before Launch:

Send your squad a personal email (not a mass blast):

Hi [Name],

The moment is almost here! [Book Title] launches on [Date], and I'd love your help making it successful.

Here's how you can help create a huge impact:

1. *Buy the book on launch day (between 12-3 PM gives maximum algorithmic boost)*

2. *Leave an honest Amazon review within the first week*

3. *Share about the book on social media (I'll provide graphics and copy)*

4. *Tell one person who would benefit from reading it*

I've attached some social media graphics and sample posts you can customize. Thank you for being part of this journey. Together, we're going to help so many people!

With gratitude,

[Your Name]

Launch Day Coordination:

Create a simple shared document with:

- Exact purchase times (choose one 3-hour timeblock for the 1st launch that gets you #1 Bestseller, then spread throughout the day for sustained ranking)

- Direct purchase link

- Sample social media posts

- Graphics in multiple formats

- Hashtags to use

When 200 people buy within a concentrated timeframe, Amazon's algorithm notices. Your book climbs the rankings. Higher rankings mean more visibility. More visibility means organic sales. The ripple begins.

The Review Strategy That Actually Works

Reviews sell books. But getting reviews is like pulling teeth, unless you have a system.

The 5-Touch System

Touch 1 (Purchase Day):

"Thank you for buying! Your support means everything."

Touch 2 (Three Days Later):

"Hope you're enjoying the book! Would love to hear what's resonating with you."

Touch 3 (One Week Later):

"Quick favour—if you've had a chance to read any of the book, would you mind leaving a review? Even two sentences help other readers discover it. Here's the direct link: [link]"

Touch 4 (Two Weeks Later):

Share a positive review someone else left. "Reviews like this make my heart sing. If you've read the book, I'd love to hear your thoughts too!"

Touch 5 (One Month Later):

Can't believe it's been a month since launch! If the book helped you in any way, would you mind sharing that in a review? Your words help others find the solutions they need."

This system gets 10x more reviews than a single ask.

The Content Multiplication Machine

Your book is a content goldmine. Every chapter can become:

10 Social Media Posts

Pull quotes, statistics, tips. One chapter = two weeks of content.

5 Blog Posts

Expand on chapter themes, add new examples, update with current events.

3 Podcast Topics

Each major concept in your chapter is a potential podcast interview topic.

1 Workshop or Webinar

Teach the chapter's content live, adding interactive elements.

1 Lead Magnet

Turn chapter exercises into downloadable worksheets.

Here's the multiplication in action:

Original Book Content:

The three types of morning routines are: Energizing (for those who need to wake up fully), Calming (for those who wake up anxious), and Productive (for those who want to maximize early hours)."

Social Post:

"Are you an Energizer, Calmer, or Producer in the morning? Your morning routine should match your natural rhythm, not fight it."

Blog Post:

"How to Choose the Right Morning Routine for Your Personality Type"

Podcast Topic:

"Why One-Size-Fits-All Morning Routines Fail"

Workshop:

"Design Your Perfect Morning: A Personalized Routine Workshop"

Lead Magnet:

"The Morning Routine Quiz: Discover Your Type"

One piece of content becomes five revenue streams and dozens of touch points.

The Podcast Tour Strategy

Podcasts sell books better than almost any other medium. One good podcast interview can drive hundreds of sales.

The Pitch That Works:

Subject: [Specific Angle] for [Podcast Name] Listeners

Hi [Host Name],

Just listened to your episode with [Recent Guest] about [Topic]. Your point about [specific detail] really resonated—it's exactly why I wrote [Book Title].

I'd love to share [specific value proposition] with your listeners. I can offer:

- *[Unique angle that fits their show]*
- *[Actionable takeaway their listeners can implement immediately]*
- *[Story or case study that illustrates the point]*

I can also provide:

- *3 potential episode titles*
- *5 suggested interview questions*

- *A free chapter of my book for your listeners*

Here's a 60-second video showing my communication style: [link]

Would this be valuable for your audience?

Best,

[Your Name]

The 50-Podcast Challenge:

Commit to booking 50 podcast interviews in your first year. That's roughly one per week. Here's the math:

- 50 podcasts with average 500 downloads each = 25,000 listeners

- 2% conversion rate = 500 book sales

- Those 500 readers each tell one person = 1,000 total impact

- The ripple continues

The Speaking-to-Book Pipeline

Every speaking opportunity, virtual or in-person, should sell books. Not through pushy sales, but through strategic integration.

The Book Table Strategy:

For in-person events:

- Beautiful table display with standing book copies

- Professional tablecloth with your logo

- Business cards, 5x7 promotional cards and bookmarks

- QR code for digital purchase

- One compelling sign: "Ask Me About [Your Book's Big Idea]"

Position yourself near the table during breaks. Don't sell; just be available for conversations.

The Virtual Integration:

For online events:

- Virtual background featuring your book cover

- Mention the book naturally within examples

- Offer a free chapter to attendees

- Include book link in your bio slide

- Host offers special bundle (your book + their product)

The Long-Game Momentum

Most book marketing advice focuses on the first 30

days. But real success comes from consistent action over months and years.

We learned this by watching author number twelve, Marcus, whose book about mindful leadership launched to exactly seventeen sales on day one. Seventeen. He was devastated. We'd done everything "right," built his squad, gathered advance praise, coordinated the launch. But seventeen sales felt like a failure.

"Keep going," we told him. "The launch is just the beginning."

He didn't believe us, but he kept going anyway. Daily posts sharing wisdom from his book. Weekly blog articles expanding on chapters. Monthly local speaking engagements at Rotary clubs, chambers of commerce, anywhere that would have him. He sent personal thank you notes to every single person who bought his book. He responded to every email, every comment, every message.

Month two: 50 sales. Month three: 150 sales. Month six: He was invited to speak at a major leadership conference. Year one: 2,000 sales and a consulting practice booked solid. Year two: A second book and a keynote at Google. Year three: International translation rights and a global consulting firm.

The seventeen people who bought on launch day? They became his most passionate advocates. One of them recommended him for that first major conference.

Another introduced him to the Google connection. Small ripples that became waves.

Month 1-3: Launch Phase

- Daily social media about the book

- Weekly podcast pitches

- Aggressive review gathering

- Book squad activation

The launch phase is about momentum. Everything should connect to your book. But here's what most people get wrong—they think "about the book" means "buy my book." Wrong. It means sharing value from the book. Teaching from the book. Telling stories from the book. The book is the source, but value is what you share.

We watched author thirty-three post "Buy my book!" every day for a month. Sales flatlined after week one. Then we watched author thirty-four share one tip from her book every day for a month, always ending with "This comes from Chapter 3 of [Book Title], available here if you want more." She sold ten times as many copies.

Month 4-6: Expansion Phase

- Weekly valuable content from the book

- Monthly speaking engagements

- Quarterly promotions

- Start gathering success stories from readers

The expansion phase is when your book starts working for you instead of you working for your book. This is when readers start sharing their transformations. Capture these stories. They're gold. One success story from a reader is worth a hundred marketing posts from you.

Simar remembers the first success story we received from one of our author's readers. The author had written about productivity for overwhelmed moms. Six months after launch, a reader sent a three-page email about how the book had saved her marriage. She'd been so overwhelmed that she was snapping at her husband, ignoring her kids, and considering leaving her job. The book's simple systems gave her breathing room. Her family noticed. Her boss noticed. Her entire life transformed.

We asked permission to share her story (anonymously). That single testimony sold more books than any advertisement could have.

Month 7-12: Authority Phase

- Position yourself as the expert on your topic

- Media opportunities

- Corporate workshops

- Plan book two

The authority phase is when you stop introducing yourself as "someone who wrote a book about X" and start being "the expert on X." It's subtle but powerful. Media starts calling you. Event planners start reaching out. You stop pitching and start selecting.

We saw this transformation with author fifty-one, who wrote about inclusive hiring practices. For six months, she pitched herself everywhere. Few responses. Then an article quoted her book. Then another. Suddenly she was "the inclusive hiring expert." Same person, same book, different positioning. She went from pitching to turning down opportunities.

Year 2 and Beyond: Legacy Phase

- Annual updated edition

- Companion products (workbooks, courses)

- Certification programs

- International translations

The legacy phase is when your book becomes bigger than a book. It becomes a methodology, a movement, a business. Not every author wants this, and that's fine. But for those who do, the book is the foundation everything else builds on.

We've watched authors turn single books into:

- Six-figure course businesses
- International speaking careers
- Consulting practices with Fortune 500 clients
- Certification programs training others in their methods
- Book series that dominate their categories

The key? They didn't see their book as the end goal. They saw it as the beginning of a larger conversation. Their book is embedded into their business strategy.

The ripple effect isn't about one big splash—it's about consistent waves that build on each other.

Everything worth doing takes time.

The Community Creation Secret

Your book shouldn't end with "The End." It should begin a relationship.

Create a simple community for your readers:

- Facebook group
- LinkedIn community

- Monthly Zoom calls

- Email newsletter

This community becomes:

- Your research lab for book two

- Your testimonial engine

- Your referral system

- Your biggest cheerleaders

One author started with 50 people in her book's Facebook group. Three years later, it has 5,000 engaged members and has become a significant revenue stream through paid memberships.

The ripple effect in action: Book creates community. Community creates connections. Connections create more readers. More readers grow the community. The cycle continues.

Breaking the Silence

RICHA PALIYA-REHAN

*Pelvic Health Physiotherapist, Women's Health
Educator, Entrepreneur & Public Speaker*

For Richa, writing *Things Every Girl Should Know About Her Body* was more than an act of authorship—it was an act of liberation. For years, she worked one-on-one with women to help them understand their bodies after a lifetime of silence, shame, and misinformation. But publishing her book gave her message wings. It turned her mission into a movement—reaching girls, mothers, and educators across the world.

"Your book isn't the end—it's the start of your movement," Samantha and Simar told her. That insight changed everything. With their support, she overcame fears about language, taboo, and perfection, and began to lead with authenticity and courage.

Today, Richa's message is sparking open, honest conversations about women's health and body literacy across generations. Her legacy is clear: knowledge is power, and understanding your body is where confidence begins.

Connect with Richa:
🌐 RichaRehan.com
✉ richa@athleticophysio.ca

Behind the Scenes to Center Stage

DANIELLE C. BAKER

*RECE, Author, TV & Podcast Host,
International Keynote Speaker*

When Danielle C. Baker began writing *Bringing Up The World: How To Finally Focus On What Matters & Watch The Child Bloom*, she saw it as a professional calling card—until it became a life-changing catalyst. As CEO of Being Connected e-Learning Inc., Danielle had long worked behind the scenes, but the process of writing her book pushed her into the spotlight, revealing a leader, advocate, and changemaker.

Partnering with Lucky Book Publishing helped her overcome the fear of visibility and claim her voice with confidence. *"Don't be the world's best secret,"* she recalls—a piece of advice that changed everything. The book became her launchpad for clarity, credibility, and connection.

Today, *Bringing Up The World* has opened international speaking opportunities, TV and podcast appearances, and collaborations that amplify her message: we can't change the world all at once, but we can do it *one child at a time*.

Connect with Danielle C. Baker:
🌐 BeingConnectedELearning.com
✉ info@beingconnectedelearning.com

CONCLUSION
Your Legacy Begins Today

You've just learned our complete system for writing and launching a book. But knowing the system and using it are two different things.

Right now, you're standing at a crossroads. One path leads back to your normal life, where this book becomes interesting information you once read. The other path leads to your published book, your message reaching people who need it, your expertise transforming lives, your community growing around shared purpose.

The difference between those paths? Action. Today. Not tomorrow, not next week, not when you feel ready. Today.

We've seen this crossroads moment hundreds of times. The authors who succeed aren't necessarily the most talented writers or the ones with the most impressive credentials. They're the ones who take the first small step, then another, then another. They're the ones who understand that a book isn't written in a day but is written day by day.

Don't do this alone. Join our private
VIP Author Community
and connect with writers around the world
LuckyBookPublishing.com/work-with-us

Your First Five Actions

Don't close this book without doing these five things:

Action 1: Write Your Why (10 minutes)

Open a document. Type: "I'm writing this book because…"
Set a timer for 10 minutes and don't stop writing until it
rings. This becomes your anchor.

Don't overthink this. Let your real reasons pour out.
Maybe it's to honor someone's memory. Maybe it's to
prevent others from making your mistakes. Maybe it's to
build the business that supports your family. Whatever
emerges, that's your truth. That's your power.

Action 2: Do the Brain Dump (30 minutes)

Get paper and pen. Write your topic at the top. Dump
everything you know about it onto paper. Stories,
concepts, examples, lessons. Don't organize—just
extract. You'll be amazed how much you already know.

We've watched hundreds of authors do this exercise. Every single one is shocked by how much content they already have. You're not starting from zero. You're starting from years of experience, learning, and living. This brain dump proves it.

Action 3: Create Your Avatar (20 minutes)

Answer the 10 avatar questions for one specific person who needs your book. Give them a name. Print their description and put it where you'll see it daily.

Make this person real in your mind. What's their morning like? What keeps them up at night? What would change if they had your solution? When you write, you'll write to them. When you build your community, you'll look for people like them.

Action 4: Start Your Squad (5 minutes)

Join one Facebook group or LinkedIn community where your ideal readers hang out. Introduce yourself. Answer one question. Plant your first seed.

This feels small, but it's huge. You're declaring yourself. You're showing up. You're beginning to build the community that will support your book and spread your message. Every author we work with says the same thing: "I wish I'd started building my squad earlier."

Action 5: Make the Commitment (2 minutes)

Send an email to someone you trust: "I'm writing a

book about [topic]. It will be published by [date]. Please ask me about my progress." External accountability transforms dreams into deadlines.

Choose someone who will actually ask. Someone who cares about your growth. Someone who won't let you off the hook. This simple email creates a contract not just with them, but with yourself.

Total time: 67 minutes. In just over an hour, you've gone from "thinking about writing a book" to "writing a book."

Your Book's Ripple Effect

Samantha here. I want to share something that happened last week. An author we worked with two years ago forwarded us an email. It was from a reader in Australia—someone we'd never met, living somewhere we'd never been.

The reader wrote: "Your book arrived at exactly the right moment. I was ready to give up on my business. Your chapter on resilience made me try one more time. That attempt worked. My business is thriving now, and I'm able to support my family in ways I never imagined. Thank you."

Our author had no idea this reader existed. The book had traveled around the world, found its way into the right hands at the right moment, and changed a life. That reader's success will impact their family, their employees, their community. The ripple continues.

This is what's waiting for you. Not fame (though that might come). Not fortune (though that's possible too). But impact. Real, meaningful, lasting impact on people you'll never meet, in places you'll never go, at moments you'll never know about.

Your book will find people in their darkest moments and offer light. It will reach someone who's been searching for exactly the solution you provide. It will validate someone who thought they were alone in their struggle. It will inspire someone to take action they've been postponing for years.

But only if you write it. Only if you share it. Only if you build the community that helps it spread.

The Community You're Joining

Simar here. When you publish your book using this system, you're not just becoming an author. You're joining a community of people who believe ideas matter, that sharing knowledge is a form of generosity, that books change lives.

This community includes:

- The entrepreneur whose book landed her a calendar full of keynote speaking stages.

- The teacher in Ontario whose book revolutionized

how schools approach early childhood development.

- The therapist in California whose book helped thousands heal from trauma.

- The executive coach in Connecticut who equips leaders to transform their life and work through the power of forgiveness.

- The mom in Toronto whose book helps parents have unshakeable bonds with their children during divorce.

Different topics, different audiences, same system, same belief: Your message matters.

But here's what's beautiful about this community: We support each other. Authors in our community beta read for each other. They share each other's launches. They celebrate wins together and problem-solve challenges together. When you write your book using our system, you're not doing it alone. You're surrounded by people who understand the journey, who've faced the same fears, who've pushed through the same doubts.

We've watched authors form mastermind groups, accountability partnerships, even business collaborations. Books that might have competed instead complement each other. Authors who might have worked in isolation instead work in community.

This is intentional. We built this system not just to help people write books, but to create connections between people with messages worth sharing. Every author brings unique expertise. Every book adds value to the collective wisdom. Every success lifts everyone.

Momentum loves company.
Write with us every Thursday at
our free Author Writing Labs.
LuckyBookPublishing.com/events

The Time Is Now

We live in an extraordinary moment in history. Never before has it been possible for anyone, anywhere, to share their message with the world. No gatekeepers. No permission needed. No limits except the ones you impose on yourself.

But this window won't stay open forever. Markets get saturated. Attention gets harder to capture. The difference between authors who succeed and those who don't isn't talent or luck—it's timing. It's starting now versus starting later.

Your ideal readers are out there right now, searching for answers you have, needing the transformation you can provide, ready for the message only you can deliver in the way only you can deliver it.

They're typing questions into Google that your book answers. They're lying awake at night with problems your book solves. They're standing in bookstores, scanning shelves, hoping to find exactly what you're going to create.

They're in Facebook groups asking for recommendations. They're on Amazon reading reviews, trying to find the book that will help. They're talking to friends, looking for solutions. Your book is the answer they're seeking, but only if it exists.

Don't make them wait.

Every day you delay is a day someone struggles without your solution. Every week you postpone is a week your message isn't spreading. Every month you wait is a month your community isn't forming.

Your Publishing Promise

If you follow the system in this book, really follow it, not just read about it, here's what we promise:

Within six months, you can have a published book. Not a perfect book (that doesn't exist), but a real book that helps real people.

Within one year, you can build an engaged community around your message. Not just readers, but people who implement your ideas, share your vision, and support each other's growth.

Within two years, your book can open doors you didn't know existed. Speaking opportunities, consulting contracts, media interviews, collaboration invitations.

Within five years, the ripple effect of your book will reach places and people you never imagined. Your ideas will be shared in conversations you'll never hear. Your solutions will help people you'll never meet. Your legacy will be established.

But it all starts with action. Today.

We're not promising it will be easy. Writing a book takes work. Building a community takes effort. Creating impact takes persistence.

We are promising it's possible. We are promising you have what it takes. We are promising the system works if you work the system.

Write the Book That Changes Everything

The title of this book isn't just about our system. It's about your book—the one you're going to write.

Your book will change everything for someone. It might be the reader who finds hope in your story. The entrepreneur who implements your strategy. The parent who discovers your solution. The professional who advances because of your insights.

But here's the secret: The book that changes everything for them will change everything for you too.

Writing a book clarifies your thinking. You'll understand your own expertise more deeply. You'll see connections you missed before. You'll articulate ideas that were fuzzy. The act of writing transforms the writer.

Publishing a book establishes your authority. You become the person who literally wrote the book on your topic. Doors open. Opportunities appear. Your voice carries more weight.

Building a community around your book creates lasting connections. You'll meet people who share your values, your vision, your mission. Some will become clients. Some will become collaborators. Some will become lifelong friends.

The ripple effect of your book extends far beyond sales and rankings. It's about impact, legacy, contribution. It's about adding your voice to the conversation. It's about sharing what you've learned so others can learn too.

Our Final Challenge

We'll leave you with the same challenge we give every author who enrolls with Lucky Book Publishing.

In the next 24 hours, tell five people you're writing a

book. Not "thinking about" writing a book. Not "planning to" write a book. Tell them you ARE writing a book.

Say the words: "I'm writing a book about [your topic]. It helps [your ideal reader] [achieve specific result]. I'm planning to publish it by [specific date]."

Their reactions will surprise you. Most will be excited. Some will want to pre-order. A few might share stories that end up in your book. All will ask you about it next time they see you, creating the accountability that transforms intention into action.

But more than that, you'll have declared yourself. You'll have claimed your identity as an author. You'll have started the ripple effect that will define the next chapter of your life.

Your Legacy Starts Now

Every book on every shelf started the same way: with someone deciding to write it. Someone who had doubts but started anyway. Someone who got stuck but kept going. Someone who feared judgment but published anyway.

Now it's your turn.

Your experiences have prepared you for this moment. Every challenge you've faced, every lesson you've learned, every success you've achieved—they've all been preparing you to write this book.

Your knowledge is needed. Someone out there is struggling with exactly what you know how to solve. They're waiting for your book, even though they don't know it yet.

Your perspective is unique. No one else has lived your exact combination of experiences. No one else can tell your story or share your insights in quite the same way.

Your book is waiting to be written. The community that will form around it is waiting to be built. The lives that will be changed are waiting for your message.

The system is in your hands. You know how to find your idea, create your outline, write your chapters. You know how to build your Book Squad, launch with impact, create ripple effects. You have everything you need.

Your squad is out there, waiting to be assembled. In Facebook groups and LinkedIn communities, in coffee shops and co-working spaces, online and offline, there are people who need what you have to offer. They're waiting for someone to lead them, teach them, show them the way. That someone is you.

Your readers are searching for what you're about to create. They don't know your name yet. They don't know your book exists yet. But they know they need help, and you have the help they need.

The only question left is: Will you begin?

Will you take the first step? Will you write your why? Will you do the brain dump? Will you start building your squad?

Will you push through the doubt, the fear, and the imposter syndrome that every author faces?

Will you trust the system, trust the process, trust yourself?

Your legacy doesn't start when your book is published. It doesn't start when you hit bestseller status. It doesn't start when your community reaches thousands.

It starts the moment you decide to write it.

It starts with the commitment to share your message.

It starts with the courage to believe your voice matters.

It starts today.

It starts now.

Welcome to the community of authors who don't just dream about writing but who write, who publish, who create ripples that change everything.

Welcome to the movement of people who believe everyone has a book in them and that book deserves to be shared.

Welcome to your new identity as an author, a leader, and a catalyst for change.

Your book is waiting.

Your community is waiting.

Your legacy is waiting.

Let's begin.

Together.

ACKNOWLEDGMENTS

To Every Author

This book exists because of every author who trusted us with their messages, their stories, and their dreams. Every question you asked, every challenge you faced, every success you achieved taught us something that made this system better.

To Our Lucky Book Publishing Community

You are not just clients... You're co-creators of this method. Your courage to share your message inspires us daily. Your willingness to be vulnerable, to share your struggles and successes and to support each other. That's what makes this more than a business. It's a movement.

To Our Families

Who supported us through late nights, working weekends, and the obsessive focus required to build something new: Thank you for believing in this vision when it was just an idea. Thank you for understanding when we missed dinners to help an author through a crisis, when we took calls during vacations because someone needed encouragement, when we poured everything into building this community.

To Our Children

Adelina, Beckham, Hamza, and Lionel, you are our greatest inspirations and the reason we believe in the power of legacy.

A special shoutout to Baby Lionel, born on the lucky day March 17, 2022 (St. Patrick's Day), whose arrival sparked the name *Lucky Book Publishing*. And to Baby Hamza and Baby Lionel, born just months apart, your tiny kicks, sweet laughter, and newfound curiosity guided us to take a leap of faith and create something far bigger than we ever imagined.

To our oldest two, Adelina and Beckham, our natural-born leaders, we are so proud of the kindness, courage, and creativity you bring to everything you do. We can't wait to see the stories inside all of you come to life one day.

From those early dreams to the ripple effect of *Lucky Book Publishing*, you have been the heartbeat behind every #1 bestseller, every author's transformation, and every story that has gone out into the world to impact millions.

You are our why, our luck, and our legacy.

To the Reader

To every person who said "I've always wanted to write a book but…", this is for you. The "but" ends now. Your story matters. Your expertise is needed. Your voice deserves to be heard.

To the authors who became our friends, who celebrated with us when things went well and problem-solved with us when they didn't: You've shown us what community really means. You've proven that when people with messages worth sharing come together, magic happens.

To everyone who shared their story with us, who trusted us with their vulnerable moments, who let us witness their transformation from aspiring writer to published author: You've given us the greatest gift. You've let us be part of your journey.

ABOUT THE AUTHORS

Meet Samantha

Samantha Moonsammy is a master connector who has spent her career bringing people and ideas together. From producing events for celebrity thought leaders to building communities of authors, she understands the power of shared wisdom. As co-founder of Lucky Book Publishing, she's helped hundreds of authors to not just write books, but build movements around their messages.

Born in Guyana and moving to Canada at age two, Samantha learned early the power of bridging cultures and bringing people together. As a natural-born teacher who set up mock classrooms with her dolls as a child, she's always been drawn to sharing knowledge and helping others grow. She lives in Ottawa with her family and is currently travelling around the world to stages, sharing the message of *Write the Book that Changes Everything.*

Meet Simar

Simar Nounou is a serial entrepreneur who believes in democratizing opportunity. With a background in digital marketing and business strategy, she saw how the traditional publishing industry left out brilliant voices and decided to create a different path. Her systematic approach to book creation has transformed "someday" authors into published thought leaders.

Growing up in Jordan after her family fled the Lebanese civil war, Simar learned resilience and independence from her father, who encouraged her to study abroad at 16. That spirit of taking on challenges and creating opportunities has driven her journey from ambitious child entrepreneur to co-founding Lucky Book Publishing. She splits her time between Toronto and Riyadh and is developing new ways to help authors build sustainable businesses around their books.

About Us

Together, we've built more than a publishing company. We've created a movement that believes everyone has a book inside them, and that book deserves to be shared with the world. Our greatest joy is watching authors discover they have more to say than they thought, build communities they never imagined possible, and create impact that ripples far beyond what they dreamed.

Find us on LinkedIn, Facebook, and Instagram at
@LuckyBookPublishing
LuckyBookPublishing.com
hello@LuckyBookPublishing.com

thank you

Thank you for reading our book!

Dear Reader,

Thank you for investing your time and energy in these pages and for trusting us to guide you on your author journey.

If something in these pages inspired you, gave you clarity, or reminded you that your story matters, we'd be so grateful if you shared that impact.

Would you take a moment to leave a review on Amazon or Goodreads?

It doesn't have to be long or polished. Just honest. Just you.

Your words help more aspiring authors find this book, believe in their own message, and take that first brave step toward writing the book that changes everything.

And if this book reminded you that your voice matters, then our mission is complete. That's what this movement is all about.

With love, belief, and gratitude,

Samantha & Simar
Co-Founders, Lucky Book Publishing

READY TO WRITE YOUR BOOK?

This book has given you our complete system, but sometimes you want support, accountability, and a community of fellow authors on the same journey.

If you're ready to turn this system into your published book, we're here to help.

Visit Luckybookpublishing.com to:

- Explore our services to help you go from idea to bestseller

- Connect with our author community

- Get personal guidance from our team

- Sign up for an upcoming writing workshop

- Access templates, tools, and resources

Your book is waiting. We'd be honored to help you bring it to life.

Remember: Opportunities come from people. When you join our community, you're not just getting a publishing system, you're connecting with hundreds of authors who will champion your message, celebrate your success, and help create the ripple effect that changes everything.

See you on the inside.

With love and anticipation for your book,
Samantha and Simar

The End

(But really, it's just the beginning...)

YOUR EXCLUSIVE BOOK BONUSES

As our gift to you, enjoy FREE access to the **Write the Book That Changes Everything digital bundle** - including the PDF of this book, the complete audiobook, author templates, and exclusive resources to help you write, publish, and promote your own bestselling book.

Simply scan the QR code below or visit **luckybookpublishing.com/book**

Because when one of us writes the book that changes everything, it creates a ripple effect that inspires the world.

www.ingramcontent.com/pod-product-compliance
Lightning Source LLC
Chambersburg PA
CBHW021146130626
46554CB00005B/1688